Stubai

PATHMASTER GUIDES

CIRCULAR 30 WALKS FROM REGIONAL CENTRES

STUBAI

John White

Series Editor
Richard Sale

The Crowood Press

First Published in 1991 by
The Crowood Press Ltd
Gipsy Lane
Swindon
SN2 6DQ

British Library Cataloguing in Publication Data
White, John
  Stubai : 30 circular walks from regional centres. –
  (Pathmaster guide series).
  1. Austria. Mountains – Visitor's guides
  I. Title   II. Series
  914.360453

  ISBN 1 85223 406 7

Picture credits
Black and white photographs throughout, and cover photographs by the author; all maps by Malcolm Walker.

In places times from timetables and certain costs, including fares, have been quoted. These were correct at time of going to press, but it cannot be guaranteed that they will remain the same in subsequent years.

Typeset by Carreg Limited, Nailsea, Bristol
Printed in Great Britain by Redwood Press Ltd, Melksham, Wilts

CONTENTS

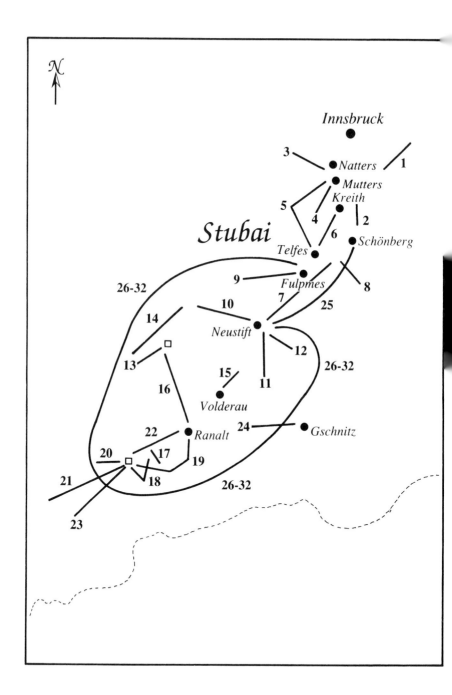

INTRODUCTION

'Gruss Gott', the greeting rang out yet again, as two cheerful hikers, ruddy faced and somewhat overdressed in heavy check shirts and tweed breeches strode purposefully past. Below us, a huge expanse of coniferous forest spread precipitously down to the valley floor, where neat meadows filled with freshly cut ricks of hay, surrounded sedate Alpine villages. Above, the high pastures soon gave way to scree and rock, while a horseshoe of great pinnacles and towers carved a jagged edge across the skyline to our right. A few minutes later, we reached the hut and drank cool beer. With the hot sun on our backs, and the hollow jangle of cowbells the only sound in the clear mountain air, it was easy to understand why people return to this area time and again.

The Stubai valley – Stubaital as it is called – is one of Austria's finest walking areas. Lying to the south of the massive Inn valley and bounded east and west by the Zillertal and Otztal Alps, it provides a mountain region of variety, quality and easy access.

There are routes and peaks for all standards. Low-level walks are popular and well-defined, often designed to make the best of the views and frequently known as Panoramawegs. The low-level scenery is both attractive and interesting, with the old wooden buildings and the old-fashioned agricultural ways proving to be as much of an attraction as the distant mountain views. Butterflies and flowers are plentiful and varied, though relatively few birds and animals are seen. (Early mornings and evenings are the best times here for nature lovers). Many of these low-level routes are suitable for young and old alike, and mountain bikers will find some excellent routes. (Notes have been included in the text where routes were thought to be particularly appropriate.)

The whole area is criss-crossed with middle- and high-level routes, often linking huts and providing well waymarked (often numbered) and entertaining walks. Many variations are possible and multi-day hut to hut excursions are commonplace. The high mountain scenery is, as one would expect, really marvellous, with views stretching far and wide from the high peaks and passes. For more experienced parties, the area's glaciers and summits give many easy grade and classic routes, with a small amount of very good rock climbing being found in the limestone areas. This outstanding variety of choice makes the Stubaital particularly attractive to families and mixed ability groups – and yet there's more. The vast majority of paths are clear, well maintained and exceptionally well waymarked, both with signing and the usual paint on rocks and trees method.

The region never seems to get overcrowded. A recent midsummer visit revealed plenty of room at campsites, pensions and hotels, a pleasant change from some of the busier Alpine areas. The only problems occurred on the busier paths at peak times, when a large number of people were walking. However, more gregarious walkers would find it acceptable. Early starts or late afternoon and evening walks mostly gave seclusion and peace.

Alongside the extensive hut system, is a useful series of chairlifts which give quick and easy access and descent from many of the popular areas. They are well run, quiet and not expensive, and even the die-hard traditionalist could find a use for some of them. Particularly useful are the lifts to the Dresdner Hütte, Kreuzjoch and Koppeneck. Watch out for closures due to maintenance, out of the main seasons.

As an extra attraction, the valley boasts year round skiing on the glacier and a popular paragliding school in Neustift. Other sporting facilities abound – you are not meant to come here for a quiet holiday! All the walks in this book can be undertaken by using private transport, the excellent bus and train service up the valley, or on foot, depending on your route. Private transport is useful but not essential.

There is an extra dimension, in addition to the variety and quality of opportunities in the outdoors – that of the valley's villages, customs and people. Many of the villages have genuine Tyrolean appeal, their ancient buildings clothed with huge murals, their woodwork intricately carved and their balconies awash with the colour of geraniums. Their charm is both relaxing and motivating. The people of the valley are as friendly and as helpful as you could hope to find, and speaking a little German goes a long way towards making friends.

Walking in Austria is certainly very different from the UK and you must make allowances and accept their way of doing things – for example, the excessive waymarking, the over-sensitive attitude to safety and the proliferation of busy huts. Having said this, the combination of the Stubaital's variety of walking, its ease of access and compact nature, superb scenery and hospitality make it a wonderful place for a walking holiday and especially good for family and mixed ability groups – after all, if you tire of walking there is always a hut round the corner where you can relax with a cool beer!

Gruss Gott.

The Grading System

Though any attempt to grade walks is to some extent subjective, I hope that the following simple system, used in conjunction with the walk descriptions, will give a reasonably accurate impression of the overall levels of difficulty of each route.

E – Easy walks which are on good tracks and which involve little height gain.

M – Longer walks which may have steep ascents and some very easy scrambling which the average walker would pass in his or her stride.

D – Routes of a harder physical nature, often involving considerable ascent gain and some scrambling which may be exposed, but still technically easy.

C – Routes which require more specialized mountaineering skills such as simple rope work and knowledge of glacier crossing. A head for heights is also an advantage.

How to get There

One of the great virtues of the Stubaital region is its proximity to the famous winter sports venue of Innsbruck. From this major city, a mere 30 minute drive leads up into the valley, a luxury which few other major Alpine areas possess. For this reason, travel by air can be very convenient. Getting there by road or rail is also quite feasible, though the drive is rather long. There are numerous package tours to Austria, some of which will come to this area. (See your travel agent).

Air

Flights to Innsbruck are available from a number of British airports, Gatwick, Southend, Manchester and Glasgow among them and a variety of options are available depending on the time of year. Charter flights are available in the winter season. Cheaper, last minute deals are available, although most of the ski related charter flights are not suitable for walkers due to the time of year. Summer charter flights are also available and over and above these options are a variety of more expensive flights. Danair, British Airways and Austrian Airlines are the main carriers. The number of flights to Innsbruck is considerably less than to Salzburg and Munich, from where trains can be caught to Innsbruck, so it is advisable to book well in advance for the flight of your choice. Flying to Frankfurt first gives a much wider choice of destinations and frequency.

From Innsbruck, a small and frequent railway service leads up into the Stubaital, terminating at Telfes (Fulpmes). A bus service continues up the valley from here. A bus service is also available from Innsbruck. Car hire and taxis are available at the airport.

Rail

A daily rail service from London Victoria to Innsbruck via Arlberg is available. However, the journey takes 22 hours, which may make flying a more favourable option. Couchettes and sleepers must be booked well in advance for journeys in the high season. If you are young enough, get an Inter Rail card which gives a month's unlimited rail travel throughout Europe. At the time of writing there is rumour of a weekly coach service to Innsbruck starting in 1990.

By Road

Although it is a long drive to this area, it is an easy one and many people will enjoy the freedom which having your own transport gives. My favourite route is to cross the channel from Ramsgate to Dunkirk and follow the toll-free autoroute past Lille into Belgium, passing Namur and continuing through Luxembourg, aiming to then bypass Saarbrucken to Pirmasens. One non-autoroute section has to be negotiated through the Rheinpfalz (a beautiful area with lots of climbing and walking and a good intermediate stop), to Llandau, but from here on, along the German autobahns past Stuttgart and Ulm, the journey is fast and comfortable. The autoroute eventually comes to an end at Kempten from where a reasonable road leads over the Fernpass into the Inn valley and its autoroute. Follow signs to Innsbruck, then the Brenner Pass. Once on the Brenner road, the Stubaital turn is just a few miles away and is clearly marked. (This short section on the Brenner route is the only charged section on this route.) Buy petrol in Belgium, Luxembourg and Germany, but not Austria and France if possible as it is considerably more expensive. It is also possible to drive through Switzerland and then via Arlberg (there is a new motorway under construction and a charge for the tunnel), or to drive down via Munich, both of which are longer – it really depends on what you want to see on your journey. Total distance from Dunkirk on the route described is about 1,005km (670 miles). Allow a full day's travel, or better still, take your time and arrive less tired.

Terrain and Climate

The Stubai valley is approximately 35km (22 miles) long and runs north-east to south-west. Its lower end, reached easily from Innsbruck, is enclosed by steep, afforested hillsides, attaining maximum heights of around 2,000m (6,500ft). As you ascend the valley, its sides become steeper and the surrounding peaks rise in height – 2,700m (8,900ft) to 2,800m (9,200ft) on Serles and the Schlicker Seespitze above Fulpmes and to between 3,300m (10,800ft) and 3,500m (11,500ft) in the cirque of peaks at the head of the valley. Subsidiary valleys run out from the main one, up to the Pinnisalm and Franz Senn huts, and give routes to the other major valleys on either side of the Stubaital, notably the Unteren and Mittleres Wipptal as well as giving access to the high peaks. At high levels, extensive glaciers are found, including that above the Dresdner Hütte which provides year-round skiing. I have concentrated on walks which for the most part avoid glacier travel, but where this is necessary, a special note has been included.

Much of the rock is gneiss, which can be loose and unpleasant, but limestone also occurs in places and gives rise to a Dolomitic type of scenery and a good variety of plant life.

In many places, the valley sides are too steep to offer routes other than on the established paths, and unless you are very experienced, too much exploration is perhaps ill-advised.

The region enjoys a typical continental Alpine climate, with reasonably sure summers and normally snowy winters. There can be great differences between the weather in Innsbruck and that on the glacier at the head of the valley – this is typical of the relatively local variations in climate experienced throughout Austria. Snow can fall at any time of the year especially at higher levels. (Neustift had snowfall during a recent visit at the end of May.) Having said that, you can normally expect spells of good weather from April through to October, though hot spells are frequently punctuated by afternoon and evening thunderstorms which can clear as quickly as they arrive. Occasional belts of poorer weather will also be found, but alongside this, there are lengthy spells of hot sunshine with valley temperatures commonly in the seventies. In winter, spells of poorer weather and snowfall contrast with settled periods of cold, clear weather. Autumn and Spring can literally have anything from hot sun to blizzards. Best time to walk? May/June (watch out for snow at higher levels) and September.

Accommodation

As tourism has been a major part of the valley's livelihood for many years, it comes as no surprise to learn that accommodation is plentiful, varied and generally of a high standard. Hotels are graded from one to five stars. At the top end of the spectrum, first-class establishments abound, and are available from Innsbruck right through to Mutterbergalm at the very head of the valley. Many have swimming pools and other sporting facilities as well as evening entertainment of varying sorts. Levels of quality and comfort are generally very high and the food is often plentiful and first rate. Prices are about what you would expect to pay for this class of Hotel, but off season bargains and other excellent deals can be found by shopping around. As much of the valley's trade revolves around skiing or summer mountain activities, some hotels will be shut outside the main winter and summer seasons. (This comment goes for all standards of accommodation.)

Middle grade hotels are also plentiful, often only differing from their more expensive neighbours in position and possession of sports facilities. Even in the middle of summer, locating suitable places presented no problem, though it would be wise to book in advance to guarantee the Hotel of your choice at the busiest times.

There are also plenty of self-catering apartments and pensions which offer excellent value for money. The self-catering option gives plenty of freedom, and on average the cost of food for a week is not much different to that at home, though individual items may be more or less expensive. Prices vary considerably in this category, so it is worth spending a bit of time looking around with the aid of the locally available information sheets (*see* page 12). As for all grades of accommodation, the prices fall into low and high season categories.

Pensions offer the best value for money for many walkers, generally being similar, but often better than our Bed and Breakfast facilities. From £6 per person it was possible in 1989 to get a most acceptable standard of room, with lots of space and unlimited hot water, though the breakfasts can be a bit dull. A word of warning – pensions close to the church in Neustift are very good, but exceptionally noisy. (The bells, the bells!)

Information on all the above types of facility is freely available from any of the information centres. Well-organised information sheets have been produced which give lists of all accommodation in the valley, together with facilities offered, number of rooms and prices for both low and high season. This is linked with a map which displays all the places on the sheet using a simple numerical key. In Neustift a huge map complete with flashing lights which illuminate individual places on request is located close to the information centre and is usable 24 hours per day. Generally speaking, this information is accurate and well worthwhile obtaining.

For some walkers, campsites and mountain huts will provide a base for part or all of their stay. There are two clean and friendly campsites in the upper part of the valley. The first, at Neustift, suffers from only one drawback – the church bells – and provides an otherwise good blend of convenience, for local amenities, cleanliness and camaraderie. Higher up the valley, the Hochstubai campsite caters mainly for caravans, but has a camping area set to one side by the river. The setting here is more rural, with a glacier river running through its centre and a huge waterfall clearly visible on the opposite side of the valley. The site has its own bar, complete with entertainment and across the road is a local's bar which is well worth a visit. This site has a peaceful setting, though shops and other facilities are a few kilometres away. Prices are the same at both sites, in 1989 it was around £3 per night.

Although no camping is officially allowed off the sites, a few miles up the valley is an area between the road and the river which is commonly used for casual camping. It has no facilities and anyone using it should take care not to leave litter or cause damage of any sort.

The network of mountain huts provides yet another form of accommodation, normally used in conjunction with a valley base. The huts are plentiful, never more than 6 hours walk apart and are generally exceptionally well equipped by comparison to other areas. Most people eat meals prepared for them at the hut, and a full rate for bed, breakfast and an evening meal with wine cost around £10 in 1989. Austrian Alpine Club and other Alpine Club members with reciprocal rights will receive a discount. Though hut facilities vary, sleeping is normally in dormitories (*matratzenlager*), but some provide smaller, bedded rooms as well. Due to the high standard and reasonable price of food in the huts, it is not normally necessary to carry a lot of food and gear whilst on hut to hut walks, making the days considerably easier. Staying in huts for at least part of the time is strongly recommended, especially outside peak periods. English is not guaranteed to be spoken, so a little knowledge of German will be useful.

There are three Youth Hostels in Innsbruck. You can get details from YHA International Travel Bureau, 14 Southampton St, London WC2.

As a summary, places to stay are plentiful, offering refreshingly good value at all standards, often with great character and local charm. Information is freely available and bookings can be made in advance through any of the tourist information centres.

You may find the following terms useful: *Zimmer frei* – rooms free (often linked with the colour green); *Fruhstucks-Pension*, or *Pension* – guest house offering rooms, breakfast and sometimes a small evening snack; and *Gasthof* and *Gasthaus* – establishments offering rooms and good eating and drinking facilities.

Getting About

Undoubtedly, one of the great advantages of the Stubai valley is its ease of access by both private and public transport. Firstly though, a general word about travelling in Austria.

Travel by rail is easy and efficient, though not always fast. The services are normally on time, clean and pass through the sort of countryside that makes leisurely travel a positive pleasure. There are different categories of trains, according to their speeds and a whole host of offers are available which make regular travelling cheaper. Besides the main line railways there are many minor, single gauge tracks which give access to some superb mountain valleys, very much like the railway into the Stubaital. If your holiday includes travel outside the Stubai area, the railway network is well worth considering.

Bus services are not perhaps as regular as in the UK, and many may have to be pre-booked during peak periods, but on the other hand, they are spotlessly clean and well maintained. They give access to large towns and remote mountain valleys alike. Large towns usually have their own well-organized bus or tram networks. As for the railways, details are available from the Austrian Tourist Offices.

Driving your own car is also a distinct possibility and roads are normally well kept, even in the mountain valleys, though they can be steep and very twisty. Speed limits are 130kph (80mph) on *autobahns*, 100kph (60mph) on other main roads and 50kph (30mph) in built up areas. Most drivers observe these speed limits strictly. Petrol is expensive – about ten per cent more expensive than in the UK, but there are only a few toll roads. In winter, snow tyres are advisable all the time, and obligatory when signed as such.

In the Stubai, these general comments for the most part apply pretty well. Travel by road is easy and uncomplicated. From Innsbruck, the Brenner Pass motorway provides the easiest approach, though there is a fee, which though not large, feels a bit steep considering the length of time you actually spend on it. The Stubaital is well signed and the road runs the full length of the valley. Although it is narrower in its upper reaches, it is never in a poor condition, and the upper part has recently been resurfaced. The main villages in the lower end of the valley have been bypassed and once you are past Neustift, there are no major settlements right through to the end of the valley. There are several garages which provide both petrol and repair facilities, including a major one on the main road 3km (2 miles) down the valley from Neustift, that is especially well equipped.

The valley has its own bus and train services. The single gauge railway which starts in Innsbruck and terminates at Telfes, near Fulpmes is an absolute delight to travel on and provides a convenient link-up for some of the walks described. The services are regular and inexpensive and at least one trip is strongly advised. The bus service runs all the way up to the very end of the road and the chairlift station, stopping at reasonably frequent intervals which are marked on the local maps. Again, some of the walks necessitate the use of this service, so it is as well to familiarize yourself with its route, stopping places and times as soon as possible. Timetables for both the bus and rail services are available from all information centres.

Another useful form of transport is the chair-lift. Scorned by some of the fittest and more enthusiastic, they prove a real benefit for most walkers, either as a quick way down at the end of a long day when knees are aching, or as a convenient method of reaching high ground quickly. The most useful ones are as follows: Mutterbergalm to Dresdner Hütte. This is open all year round to serve the skiing on the glacier as well as walkers. Neustift to just below the Elferhütte. This is open in winter for skiers and most of the time from May to October for walkers, climbers and paragliders. From July to September, opening times are 8a.m. to 5p.m., at other times 8.30a.m. to 4.30p.m. Fulpmes to Kreuzjoch. This is a long, slow lift offering great views. Its opening times similar to the last lift. It is highly recommended. Mieders to Koppeneck. Another summer lift which gives access to a fine, lower-level walking area. If you are going to make fairly regular use of the lift system, it is worth getting a Gastekarte, which entitles you to a reasonable discount.

Mountain bikes also provide a good means of transport, and are popular both on the roads and on the many well surfaced forest tracks. They are available for hire in all the major centres. If in doubt, ask at one of the very helpful information centres.

Money

The Austrian unit of currency is the schilling, each one of which is divided into 100 tiny groschen. As a guide, in 1989, the exchange rate was AS20 to £1, though this does vary – for example in 1981, there were AS60 to £1! Banknotes are being replaced frequently, and some notes are out of date and will not be accepted except at certain banks. It is worth checking initially to ensure that some crafty shopkeeper does not fob you off with an outdated note.

Both foreign currency and Austrian schillings may be brought into the country in unlimited amounts, and although there is a limit of AS50,000 for taking out of the country, this does not apply to foreign currency.

Money can be exchanged at all banks and also at exchange bureaus and many tourist offices. Opening hours of all these establishments vary, so it is worth checking on arrival to ensure that you can always change money if you need to. Sunday is a difficult day, some tourist offices change money only in the early morning, and banks and other agencies are shut. Also, check on public holidays, as change facilities may not be available on these dates. Both travellers cheques and cash are easily changed, though for safety reasons, travellers cheques are obviously advisable. Credit cards are widely accepted except perhaps at smaller hotels and many places, though by no means all, will accept Eurocheques.

The Law for Walkers

All the walks described in this guide are on paths which are in regular use and which are well marked. As such, there should be little need for users of it to stray beyond the routes described. The vast majority of other paths to which the public have access are also well defined and waymarked, so there is little need to walk anywhere except in the right places. It will soon become obvious if you are in the wrong place – it will either be unnavigably steep or very clearly lead to private dwellings. If someone is really determined to keep you out, the words Verboten, Privat or Privatweg will soon be seen.

Like many aspects of Austrian life, walking is extremely well organized by comparison with the UK and there are always plenty of signals which ensure that walkers keep on the right routes. Above and beyond this, you are not likely to be prosecuted if you inadvertently go the wrong way. More likely, the right way will be politely pointed out to you, or the offer of passage made in a friendly manner. It is worth remembering that walkers have used this valley for many years and the locals are quite used to them.

Perhaps the most important consideration is to follow some sort of country code – your own version of any of the popular codes will suffice. Perhaps the main point is to respect the life of the countryside – in this way you will automatically consider all the other parts of the code.

Avoid unnecessary noise
Do not leave any litter
Do not pick flowers or plants
Do not disturb wildlife
Re-close all gates and avoid climbing fences or walls
No smoking or fires in the forests
Keep to footpaths
Love and respect nature

The attitude of respect towards nature is very important and is stressed at many of the entry points into the mountains. Above and beyond this, make sure that your activities do not conflict with the use of the land for agriculture – and remember that virtually every bit of land is used for something. As a generalisation, if you behave and react sensibly and with consideration, you will have few problems.

Clothing and Equipment

The vast majority of walks in this book can be tackled with the sort of equipment that should be worn and carried for summer mountain walking in the UK. Where other, more specialised items are required, a note is made at the start of the route description.

An absolutely huge range of outdoor gear is now available. In recent years, it has become ever more colourful and fashionable, whilst generally retaining good levels of performance. My overall advice is to shop carefully, get what you want, and not what the shop assistant wants to get rid of, and buy the best gear you can afford – it will perform better and last longer.

Essential Items

Boots   Light to middle weight, tough enough to stand the sort of terrain you generally walk in. This is a crucial buy, so go to your absolute limits of expenditure and make sure they are well worn in before your holiday. High quality, fell-running type trainers are a good alternative.

Rucksack   Ideally a 30 – 45-litre daysack. It is a good idea to place the contents in a plastic liner to ensure that they do not get wet.

Waterproofs   A breathable material such as Gore-tex is ideal, especially for summer temperatures. Light overtrousers are recommended for the higher-level walks. Whatever you choose, it is important to have something.

Compass   The Silva type is good. Knowing how to use it is essential.

Map   The right area, preferably 1:25,000, plus the ability to use it.

Plastic Whistle   The international distress signal is six blasts per minute, repeated.

First-aid kit   Sun cream, insect repellant, triangular bandage, plasters, large field dressing, crepe bandage, pain killers.

Survival bag   Large polythene survival bag – a life saver.

Food and drink   What you take depends upon the route chosen, whether you plan to use mountain restaurants and so on. Summer conditions can be very hot, and at higher altitudes than normal, dehydration is the biggest problem. Drink plenty and make sure that you are carrying at least a litre per person. It is worth carrying some high energy emergency food such as chocolate or nuts. This should be for emergency use only – if your levels of temptation are low, do as a friend of mine did and carry something you don't like (in his case it was dates). In this way, you won't eat them unless it is a real emergency!

Clothing   Very much up to the individual, but I recommend shorts plus tracksuit bottoms, or breeches, T-shirt, cotton ski type shirt and a pile jacket, plus waterproofs. Several thin layers are preferable to one thick one, and exactly what you take will depend on the weather and the nature of the walk. Higher-level walkers will find a hat, gloves, a spare jumper and socks useful.

Extras   Many Austrian walkers use sticks, sometimes excessively and incredibly large ones. If you think a stick is a good idea for you, try ski sticks – the adjustable length ski mountaineering type are excellent and mountain walkers throughout the Alps use them. Sunglasses are an often overlooked item, and are an absolute must if there is any snow about. If you take a camera, remember to take a spare film. Early and late season walkers may wish to take a torch. The Petzl-type-head torch is best and remember the spare battery and bulb. A phrase book and/or a dictionary will also be useful to some.

As a general rule, I try to travel as light as possible, and on hot, sunny summer days it is possible to travel on many of the easier walks with minimum gear.

Food and Wine

Although the Stubai does not offer the variety of eating that can be found further east in Austria, it shares with other parts of the country a reputation for good quality and generosity of portion which makes it a fine eating area. As a new arrival, it might be easy to imagine that you had stumbled upon a particularly generous establishment, but in truth, virtually everywhere provides good food and plenty of it – the average Austrian has a hearty appetite. Weight-watching is probably the only problem you will encounter.

If you are cooking your own food, you will find a good variety of products available in the supermarkets, at prices which work out on average, very similar to those in the UK. It does pay to shop around though, as prices do differ slightly, and equally importantly the quality and variety of produce may vary between establishments. Meats tend to be dear, but fresh produce is well priced.

For many people, it will be as convenient to eat out in one of the many restaurants, gasthofs and pensions which offer this facility. Excellent meals can be had at some of the humblest looking pensions for around £5 for a three course meal, even a little less in places. Set menus are very popular and are usually excellent value for money, the hearty portions being very suitable for hungry walkers. Soups are very popular at all levels of restaurant, such as *leberknodlsuppe*, a meat broth with liver dumplings, or *gulaschsuppe*, a goulash stew. Veal and beef are the dominant meats. *Wiener schnitzel*, normally a well-prepared veal steak is popular, as are the many other types of *schnitzel* commonly available. Chips, or *pommes frites* are commonly served as are other forms of potato, which will contain the word *kartoffeln* in them somewhere. Mixed salads are popular and are commonly known as *gemischter salat*. Menus are often in more than one language, and in any case, it is always quite exciting to order in complete ignorance as this is guaranteed to lead to experimentation! As a generalization, you are not likely to get anything which is unpalatably rich or hot, and food-lovers will have great fun.

One other Austrian speciality is the cake-shop, or *konditorei*. These places are unique to Austria and provide a variety and quality of pastries and cakes which is difficult to ignore.

Austrian wines are not that well known by French or even German standards. However, don't be fooled by this, as Austria does have its own excellent wines. The better ones tend to be white and on the dry side (the climate apparently makes red wines more difficult to make), and they tend to be drunk when young. Wines from other countries are also commonly found, but local wines, where available are strongly recommended.

The best tip I could give to any about eating and drinking in the Stubai is to try the most local looking places possible, ignore the Pizzerias (though they do perfectly good food), and experiment as much as possible. Much of the enjoyment is in the discovery of the new.

Glossary

Konditorei   Cafe for excellent cakes, snacks and drinks.
Gasthof/Gaststatte   Restaurant offering snacks and meals, often traditional and with good ambience.
Imbiss   Snack bar.
Restaurant   Restaurant for full meals, often with International as well as local cuisine.
Was kostet das?   How much is that?
Getranke   Drinks.
Fruhstuck   Breakfast.
Fleisch   Meat.
Fisch   Fish
Kase   Cheese

Preparation Before You Go

The preparation and planning of your visit to the Stubai will no doubt begin with long hours spent examining maps, reading guides, looking at photos and imagining what it will be like to actually be there. Flights and holidays will be checked, price for price, quality against quality. Should you drive and maybe hire a car when you are there? All this background information is vitally important as it will give you a good idea of what to expect when you get there, and ensure that you choose the right sort of a visit for your needs.

Only you can decide exactly which is going to be most suitable, but here are some tips which may come in handy.

British citizens require no visa or health documents.

A full UK citizen's passport or a British Visitor's passport will be acceptable in Austria. The former is only available in regional passport offices (allow plenty of time) and the latter from post offices, but only lasts for one year.

Insurance is obviously a must, and check that whichever policy you choose, it covers you for the activities you will be involved in. For example, will it cover Mountain Rescue bills? The British Mountaineering Council, based in Manchester provides a good insurance cover for walkers and climbers. Tour operators will offer sound insurance and you may be able to use part of a home insurance policy. If in doubt, double check and get the right one to cover all eventualities. There too many available to go into any detail here.

Maps can be bought at good book and mountaineering shops, though they sometimes have to be ordered. Remember that the larger scale maps are advisable for walking, whilst a smaller scale may be useful for covering the whole area on one sheet, but in less detail. Excellent maps suitable for walking at 1:30,000 can be purchased locally under the name *Kompass Wanderkarte*. A good idea would probably be to buy a small scale map before you go, and get the large scale local maps on arrival, though some people will wish to have the lot before departure.

If you are travelling by car, you will need your driving licence and registration documents, and Green Card insurance is recommended but not obligatory. You must have a first-aid kit, a set of spare bulbs and a red warning triangle which must be placed on the roadside 50m (160ft) behind the car in the event of a breakdown.

As a general rule, prepare as much as possible before you go, travel as light as possible and spend a good amount of time in planning – it is time well spent.

Health Hazards

Hazards of this nature are fortunately few. But watch out for stomach problems caused by the rich and plentiful supplies of food served, although those used to a hearty and mixed diet should have no problems at all. Main problems are likely to be experienced in the mountains.

At any time of the year, the opposing complaints of heatstroke/heat exhaustion and exhaustion/exposure could be problems. In summer, the heat can be intense, even at height, and allowances should be made for this. Water loss through sweating and evaporation can be very high and the most important thing is to get used to the heat gradually and to up your intake of liquid. This applies especially on the higher-level walks, where the increased altitude accelerates dehydration. A good diet, plenty of liquid and a sensible approach to walking should alleviate any potential problems. If you are susceptible to the sun, walk early or late, wear a broad brimmed hat and wear good sunglasses. Keep skin covered up, or expose very gradually – the high mountain sun is very powerful.

The problems of exposure, or hypothermia are well known. A combination of factors such as inadequate diet or lack of sleep, combined with high energy exercise and intense cold can lead to a combination of exhaustion and chilling which if untreated can lead to death. Classic conditions are when the victim becomes wet and strong winds contribute to the quick removal of body heat. Extremities become cold, as body heat is concentrated on vital organs and the casualty becomes shivery, slow, quiet and may exhibit uncharacteristic tendencies such as sweating. If you suspect a member of your party is succumbing to this condition, stop immediately, get them in shelter (polythene survival bag for example) and warm with another person, hot drinks and food. Do not rub or give alcohol as this has the effect of removing body heat from the vital organs to the surface of the body, thus accelerating the heat loss. Further walking or effort will also contribute to heat loss, so only walk the victim down if the valley or a chairlift is close by. Prevent exposure by tackling suitable walks, keeping to a good diet (high available carbohydrate), wearing good clothing, including hat and gloves and keeping dry. Remember that if one member of the party is suffering, others could be as well.

Altitude is another potential problem on the higher walks. Above approximately 2,500m (8,200ft), some people will experience increased tiredness and thirst, possibly head and stomach aches, especially when physically exerting themselves. Acclimatization at this altitude is normally very quick and a couple of trips to this height or above will usually sort the problem out.

Minor problems such as blisters can easily be remedied as long as they do not become too bad, so carry a small first aid kit (*see* the section on clothing and equipment).

The People and the Country

It's a well known fact that despite its relatively small size, Austria packs within its borders more superb mountains, lakes, forests and beautiful cities than countries many times its size. Its attractions are compact and easily reached – no one could call Austria's countryside boring. In addition to this, it can boast a population which is friendly and welcoming, which cares about its environment and demands the highest standards in facilities and comfort. The Austrians will take your money, but they will do it with a smile and leave you feeling that you actually got something worthwhile for it.

The country is shaped like a pork chop, the narrow end of which points west and contains the Tyrol region within which the Stubai is situated. As in many other Alpine countries, there is a marked difference between the way of life in the high mountain valleys and that in the larger cities, in particular the capital, Vienna, though there are obviously many common factors. For example, Austria is a bastion of the Catholic faith, town and country alike.

Austria's economy is as buoyant as it ever has been and the standards of living are generally comfortable, moving towards luxurious for some. The country is clean and well cared for, reflecting the caring nature of its inhabitants, though as in any part of the world, some places are worse than others. What you will not find anywhere in this region is the sort of litter-ridden squalor so common in many British cities.

The mountainfolk tend to be traditionalists, especially in the older age group. Traditional dress is worn frequently – mostly on Sundays though not always so, and some people will be found wearing traditional dress in the Stubai, as a matter of course. The valley population is generally very friendly, but often polite almost to the point of being stand-offish at the same time. The ability to speak a little German comes in very handy indeed. In all my experience of climbing and walking in the Alps, I can honestly say that nowhere has provided the same feelings of friendliness and charm, and it is easy to feel very much at home here. Having said that, it pays not to be too familiar, and to adopt their ways of politeness and good manners, being formal rather than too easy going.

In the mountains, almost every person greets and is greeted with *gruss gott* (rough translation may God go with you), though the standard *guten tag*, or abbreviated *tag* is also used as hello. The well-known phrase *auf wiedersehen* means goodbye. Yes is *ja*, pronounced yar and no is *nein*, pronounced as the number nine. *Bitte* means both please and you are welcome or okay and thank you is *danke*.

THE WALKS

Walk 1   Schloss Ambras – Muhlsee – Lanser See – Igls

Map no:	Kompass 1:25,000; Stubaital
Walking time:	2 hours 30 minutes
Grading:	E
Highest altitude:	880m (2,890ft)
Lowest altitude:	580m (1,900ft)

A very pleasant walk with historical interest and a return journey by train. It can be usefully combined with a visit to Innsbruck, especially when the weather is bad up in the mountains. It can be done in reverse, in which case the start point is the railway station on the outskirts of Igls, on the road to Lans. Doing the walk this way is easier, due to the fact that it is downhill. There is approximately 290m (950ft) height difference.

The Walk

The village of Ambras is the starting point and it is easily reached by bus from the main Innsbruck station with departures every 30 minutes or by car from Innsbruck or the Stubai valley through Igls and Lans. The walk starts splendidly, with a compulsory visit to the magnificent castle of Schloss Ambras, which is open 10a.m. – 4p.m. (except Tuesday), from May to September. It is one of the finest and best preserved castles in Austria and was originally a Gothic castle built by the Duke of Andechs in the eleventh century. It was then rebuilt as a residence for the Archduke Ferdinand of

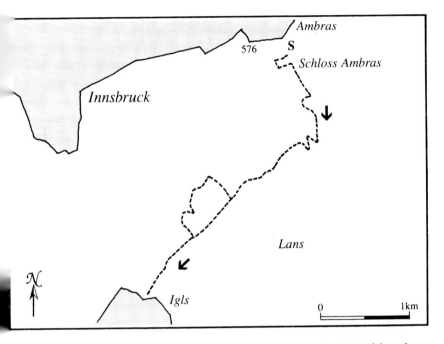

Tyrol in the German Renaissance style between 1564 and 1582. Although the bulk of the Duke's personal collection of fine art was long since transferred to the Kunsthistorisches Museum in Vienna, there is still a very large collection of pictures, armour and weapons, furniture and a variety of medieval curiosities. The grounds of the castle are both beautiful and extensive and are probably best viewed in early autumn. They contain the original jousting area, and a small cemetery containing heroes of the War of Liberation. In summer, concerts are held in the castle's main hall. One thing most visitors will remember, is the bath which belonged to Phillipine Wetser, the wife of Archduke Ferdinand II. The rumour was at the time that she had been murdered in this huge vessel, which is copper lined, measures 2 x 3m (6 x 9ft) and holds 810 litres (180 gallons) of water. Fortunately, the rumour was not true.

From the castle, follow the road to the first right bend and follow a path which leads past the disused pool and rejoins the road. Then, before the bridge, there is a gateway which gives access to open fields that lead across to the edge of the forest. Cross the railway, steadily ascending all the while, to reach the golf course and the Sperberegg. A short way after the Golfplatz and high above the Muhlsee, a right turn is taken, the start of a loop which eases a way through pleasant woodlands and eventually curls around the

The Lanser See

Lanser See – a popular haunt for Innsbruck's summer bathers – before rejoining the railside path. This part of the route is likely to be very busy during the day, with walkers, joggers and cyclists sharing the wide forest tracks. It's still a relatively peaceful place however, and it is not difficult to slip off the main paths to find somewhere quiet. By the Lanser See, a lakeside café offers refreshments, and the route continues along the edge of the lake before veering off and ascending slightly to regain the railway. There is an interesting house on this last section, whose roof resembles the hull of a boat – maybe it is! It's also quite noticeable here, that there is a very different attitude towards access, with many places proudly displaying aggressively worded signs which leave no doubt as to where you shouldn't be. This, coupled with some fearsome looking spike-topped fences and equally fearsome sounding dogs makes a stark contrast to the gentle ways in which walkers are kept on the right track up in the Stubai.

The final stretch of the path lies alongside the little railway line, terminating just before the centre of Igls, at the entrance to the Wipp valley. Situated 333m (1,093ft) above the city of Innsbruck, Igls is a well-known winter sports centre and is well worth a look round if time permits. One attraction is the Patscherkofel cable-car which runs from the village to the top of the Patscherkofel mountain at just over 2,000m (6,600ft) in less than

20 minutes. The half-way stage is Heiligwasser (Holy Water), which has a spring said to be a panacea for all ills. Views from the summit over the Inn Valley and the city are excellent. Beyond Innsbruck are the Karwendel, to the north-west is the Miemingers, and north of them the Zugspitze, marking the border with Germany. To the south-west can be seen many of the Stubai's glaciers, whilst to the south-east the nearer peaks are the Tuxer Alps, and beyond are the Zillertal Alps. There is plenty of walking, including the Zirbenweg, a long and well-marked trail leading east from the cable-car station.

Igls itself has plenty of shops and bars, if you feel a sudden need for this sort of attraction, and is not an unpleasant place to spend an afternoon. When the sightseeing is over, the return journey down to Schloss Ambras is best done by train, a relaxing and scenic ride which rounds off the day nicely.

Walk 2   Innsbruck – Stefansbrucke – Telfer Wiesen – Innsbruck

Map no:	Kompass 1:25,000; Stubaital
Walking time:	3 hours (including rail and bus journeys but not to look around Innsbruck)
Grading:	E
Highest altitude:	1,000m (3,280ft)
Lowest altitude:	720m (2,360ft)

The Walk

Innsbruck is generally recognized as the capital of the Tirol, and it must be one of the most beautiful towns of its size anywhere in the world. Lying in the flat Inn valley, its surroundings can hardly be faulted. To the north the bleached white and grey peaks of the Karwendel, whilst to the south the Stubai and Tuxer ranges rear up ever more steeply, topping out in bright, eye-narrowing glaciers.

Innsbruck is reckoned to be 750 years old – it received its municipal charter in 1239 – and it has great historical importance as a crossroads between Germany and Italy and Austria and Switzerland. Its old centre which is very Baroque in style has remained virtually complete – only the high-rise skyline has changed much and there are many things to do and see. In fact, the centre of Innsbruck is quite compact and sightseeing is considerably convenienced by virtue of this. Many of the most beautiful buildings in the town were built by Emperor Maximilian or by Empress Maria Theresa, who gave her name to the town's main street – a good point at which to make a start. Maria-Theresien-Strasse runs north/south, is the main shopping centre and from its environs can be found some of the most worthwhile sights hereabouts. Around half-way down this famous street, face north and you will see one of the best mountain views of any city, up towards the Nordkette. Innsbruck also possesses the famous Golden Roof – the Goldenes Dachl. To see this, go to the bottom of the street and locate Herzog Friedrich Strasse. Walk down this and at its end this popular sight lies across the other side of

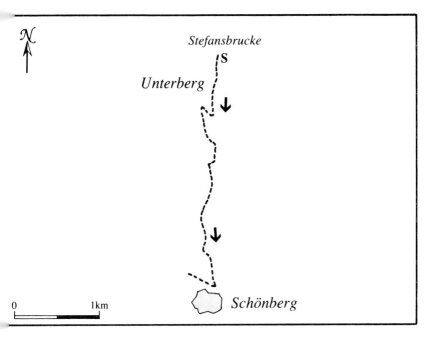

the little square. And no, it's not really gold, but gilded copper tiles which shimmer and gleam and produce a fair copy. There are many other superb buildings and magnificent examples of architectural splendour to be seen – the nearby Helbinghaus and Goldener Adler, one of the oldest inns in Innsbruck (sixteenth century), the Imperial Church and adjoining Silver chapel, the Hofburg Palace with its beautifully laid out Imperial Gardens and so on and so forth. The best way to enjoy these many and varied delights is to make a visit to the Information Centres at Bozner Platz 6 or Burggraben 3, and make best use of the information and expert advice available. No one could be disappointed with a day in Innsbruck.

After a look around the city, the walk commences by first locating the main bus station in Innsbruck. From here, a regular bus service runs up into the Stubai valley (exact times vary according to the time of year, so check first). Our destination is Stefansbrucke – Stephen's Bridge. Though dwarfed by the newer Europa Bridge which carries the Brenner Pass motorway, the arch of Stefansbrucke is nonetheless an impressive sight. It was built in 1845 when the Brenner road was relocated to the east side of the Burgstall below Schönberg. It spans the Reutzbach as a 45m (148ft) long, 36m (118ft) high structure which must have been as impressive in its day as the Europa Bridge is now.

A forest track near Telfer Wiesen

The drop off point in Stefansbrucke is the Inn, from where you walk due south, soon passing the houses of Unterberg. Beyond here is the church, in front of which you turn right and ascend past the sawmill, soon crossing a footbridge across the Reutzbach. Then, climbing up through deciduous woodland for a change, follow a rather overhung path on to a good forest road. Views back down into the valley start to open up and the motorway is ever conspicuous but rarely a real nuisance. Pleasant contouring along a gentle forest track then leads to a junction, at which we turn up to the right, following a path which runs up through the woods and then open meadows to reach the railway line and the station known as Telfer Wiesen. This is a fine spot to picnic, the views across the Serles being superb and the overall mood of the place being slow and lazy. Even the train seems this way, moving ponderously, reminiscent of a long gone age when time had a different meaning. It's quite easy to feel that time has slowed down – if only the trains kept running all night!

There are options from here. The simplest is to hop on to the train (don't forget to wave it down) and enjoy the gentle 40-minute ride back to Innsbruck. The alternative is to consider extending the walk a little, and you have a choice of walking up track or down track. Walking up track leads to the termination of the railway at Telfes and the path is easy, flat and offers increasingly fine views of the upper part of the Stubai valley. (To get on to this or the down track route, cross the railway line and the track is virtually immediately above it). If you turn right and walk down track, you will follow a good path which contours above the railway line and passes a fine iron viaduct (this looks particularly fine when the train crosses it). This route leads to Kreith and another stopping point for the railway.

Whichever route you take, the most important consideration is to ensure you plan your day in advance, so that you can make best use of your time in Innsbruck and allow time for a relaxing afternoon (or morning) on this highly attractive and endearing walk. It is a route which obviously provides an alternative to higher-level walking when the weather is bad, but on a bright, settled day even the most hardened Alpiniste who longs for high, cold glaciers and lichen-streaked rock will reap some cultural reward, and families and non-Alpinistes will enjoy a day to be remembered.

Walk 3   Mutters – Neugotzens – Natters – Mutters

Map no:	Kompass 1:25,000; Stubaital
Walking time:	2 hours
Grading:	E
Highest altitude:	830m (2,720ft)
Lowest altitude:	738m (2,421ft)

It is a good idea to take swimming costumes if the weather is good!

The Walk

This gentle walk is situated right at the lower end of the Stubai valley, in an area strictly known as the Unteren Wipptal. Its atmosphere and character is very different from the high mountain walks. This is no loss however, and the route is excellent for families or for a gentle day, compensating for the lack of steep rock faces and precipitous paths by virtue of the marvellous forests, charming villages and ever-changing views.

Mutters, the starting point, is best reached either by car or by the Stubai railway. It is essentially an old farming village which has done well to maintain its country air despite the impact of tourism, and it is well worth extending your time here to spend a while in the town itself. Indeed, the town boasts that it has twice been awarded the prize for the most beautiful Tyrolean village and also the 'quality seal' for its environment. The centre-piece of the place is its church, complete with huge green spire, whose architecture is so characteristic of the Baroque style commonly found in this region. From the central part of the town, the first part of this walk takes the road which leads westwards, first crossing the Stubai railway line, and then immediately passing a football ground on the right. The path which leaves the roadside is difficult to locate, especially when the vegetation is high, but the best way to find it is to walk about 150m (500ft) from the football ground to the point on your left, at which the roadside woodland ends. At this point, a small path can be seen leaving the road, and working a way back up to the left through the woodland. After a few minutes, it

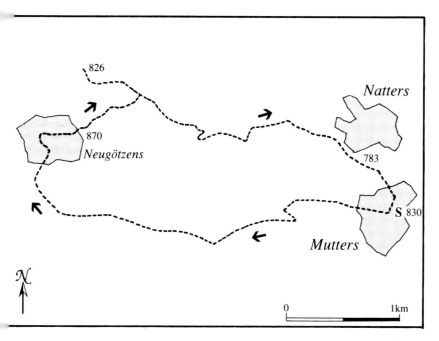

eases and meets another path, the Panoramaweg, which is signed. At this
junction is another church – this time one which is definitely not in any
sort of traditional style!

We turn right here, and follow a good track (the typical Panoramaweg),
which contours above the valley. When gaps in the forest permit, there are
wonderful views over the Inn valley to the Karwendel and to the Nordkette.
Closer by, the valley is cultivated with crops which are not seen higher up
the Stubaital such as maize – evidence of the different and more sheltered
climatic conditions found down here. The Panoramaweg is also an excellent
wildlife area, the forest composition being more varied than in many other
areas, and with more gaps, providing more light for ground cover plants and
shrubby growth. The sunny glades have more than their fair share of
butterflies and we saw huge emerald green dragonflies, almost as big as small
birds. The flight patterns of these creatures are truly amazing. They seem
able to convert fast forward flight to a stationary hover instantly, and to
resume a fast speed equally quickly. There is also a very wide variety of
woodland plants here, certainly more so than anywhere else, including many
species which would commonly be found in the UK. If you can find a good
reference book on any aspects of wildlife here, it would be worth taking on
this walk.

Mutters

The Panoramaweg eventually descends to meet the road. Cross this by the bus stop and go down a short way to a T-junction. Turn right here and walk through a residential area (this is Neugotzen) to another T-junction. Turn left here and follow the winding road down through a dark forest area to a 'multi-junction'. A short way to the left from here is the Natterer See, a small lake which is a popular goal for the inhabitants of Innsbruck during the hot summer months. There is also a campsite here, which would be a good base for the lower part of the valley, though out of the main season this area can be virtually deserted.

Returning to the 'multi-junction', imagine you have just arrived from your original point of entry and turn right, subsequently following the right fork where the road splits again. After about 200m (200yds) along this road, a path leads off to the right which is signed Herrnsteig Natters. This part of the walk is as pleasant as any other on this route, climbing gently through the forest before traversing and eventually descending into Natters. From the centre of Natters, take the minor road which leads to the south-east. This soon climbs quite steeply, crosses the Stubai railway again and then leads almost immediately back into the centre of Mutters.

Walkers used to a diet of high mountain paths, scree and ice would be well advised to consider an occasional change of staple food, and try the lower level walks such as this. The ambience, the increased amount and variety of wildlife and the charming towns are as much a part of the character of the Stubaital as the higher regions, and are well worth experiencing.

The roads which follow a similar line to the paths would make a pleasant cycling route, though the walk described is not recommended for mountain bikes.

Walk 4   Mutters – Raitiser Alm – Kreither Alm – Kreith

Map no:	Kompass 1:25,000; Stubaital
Walking time:	3 hours 30 minutes
Grading:	M
Highest altitude:	1,153m (3,783ft)
Lowest altitude:	830m (2,720ft)

A middle-level walk with plenty of interest and no problems as far as the terrain is concerned. The whole route can be done in training shoes as the paths are so well maintained. Having said that, there is around 720m (2,360ft) of ascent involved, so it's not easy going all the way!

The Walk

Starting in the centre of Mutters, which may be reached by car, bus or Stubai railway, locate the road which runs parallel to the road to Kreith in a south westerly direction. If you've picked the right route you will soon cross over the Stubai railway line, and then shortly after this a path leads off to the left, crossing the railway line again twice, and rising to join a better track which comes in from the left. From here, you have a gentle climb through the forests to the Scheipenhof at 1,130m (3,707ft).

The ascent is never too steep, but relentless nonetheless, and it is a good thing that periodic gaps in the wall of dark green trees give opportunities to spend a few minutes resting and looking out over the Inn valley, where the views to the east of Innsbruck and of the city itself are particularly good. Whilst ambling up through these great forest areas, it is worth remembering just how important they are to Austria's economy. Approximately one quarter of all Austrians earn a living from the forests, which in turn cover forty-four per cent of the country's land surface, one of its great natural resources. In fact, its economic importance is only surpassed by the forests of two other nations, Finland and Sweden. So, the woodlands are far more important than they may initially appear, and you will no doubt see plenty of evidence

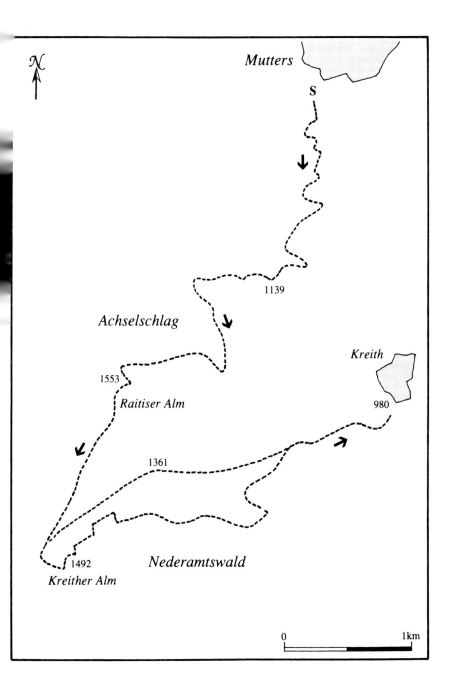

Mutters

S

1139

Achselschlag

Kreith

1553

980

Raitiser Alm

1361

Nederamtswald

1492

Kreither Alm

0   1km

of forestry work on your travels. Most of them are well managed, with recreational provision given a high degree of importance. The only negative comment I would have is that they are often rather too uniform in terms of their species distribution, and it would be good to see more attempts at integrating a greater proportion of deciduous species, which in turn tend to increase the amount of wildlife.

Coniferous trees which you will commonly see include the Stone Pine (*Zirbe*). The Stone Pine, growing at higher levels and often in exposed places where little else will survive, is often wind battered, stunted and twisted. Its smooth wood is used for carving and for rustic furniture. Various spruces are very common in the main forests; known as *fichte*, they produce a very resonant wood which is used for sounding boards in pianos and for manufacturing the bodies of violins. Larch is also frequently seen. The only conifer to shed its needles in winter, larch is a rather rough and tough wood. However, it adds a welcome touch of colour to the uniformity of the forests, turning many shades of yellow, gold and brown in the autumn, and brightening the scenery in spring, when the new needles are a bright, vibrant and fresh green.

In the undergrowth of this forest, you will see many plants – bracken (which fortunately keeps to the forests here), male fern and equisitales, or horse tails and you will also see some fine beech trees. Where the forest paths are wide, and light is allowed to penetrate the canopy of dark needles, extensive regeneration of young trees can be seen – a sign of what would happen in other areas if spaces were created.

Continuing up from the Scheipenhof, some long, straight sections of track and a final couple of hairpins lead thankfully to the Raitiser Alm – even though the ascent is not steep, it is unrelenting and quite tiring. The hut is beautifully situated, tucked charmingly into a clearing in the forest with an open meadow stretching out to its front. This hut has a different character to most, being very much in the forest, and without the exposed position which usually gives rise to fine views. Despite this, it is a pleasant place to stop and pursue the most popular Austrian pastimes which seem to be eating and drinking.

The next goal is Kreither Alm. A narrow path leads off to the rear of the Raitiser Alm and follows a traverse line across the hillside (the worst path on the route), before joining up with a better track, which is followed down to a junction. From here, it is possible to see the Brenner Motorway and its Europa bridge – one of the most impressive anywhere. Looking across to the river bed, a huge quantity of pale grey scree has been washed down from the lower reaches of Saile (Nockspitze), which is quite startling in its sheer

Stockerhof

volume. Ignore the turn to the left here and continue uphill for a short way before traversing round to the hut, which can easily be seen through the trees from the original junction. Another forest track leads from this hut down towards the Stockerhof, but before then, fork left at a junction which leads back down into the valley bottom and then eventually to Kreith. From here, the best way to return to Mutters is via the railway, a gentle end to the walk and an ideal opportunity to wind down and relax and to admire the fine views down into the main valley.

Although many of the tracks in this area are good for mountain bikes, the section to the rear of the Raitiser Alm would be less than ideal, and adventurous riders are left to plan their own routes. If you're into running this is a good route, with gentle gradients and a mixture of cool forests and interesting views.

Walk 5 Mutters – Mutterer Alm – Birgitzkopflhütte – Saile – Pfarrachalm – Telfes

Map no:	Kompass 1:25,000; Stubaital
Walking time:	5 hours (if chair-lift is used)
Grading:	D
Highest altitude:	1,153m (3,783ft)
Lowest altitude:	830m (2,720ft)

This is quite a long route, even if the chair-lift is used for the initial part of the ascent. The views are outstanding, especially from the summit and the walk is highly recommended.

The Walk

In good conditions, the Mutters area becomes a delightful winter venue, with an interesting variety of ski runs and added attractions such as toboggan runs, an ice rink and so on. Add to this the true Tyrolean charm of the village itself, and you have a first class, though small resort which unlike many others, hasn't sacrificed too much in pursuit of customers. One of the spin-offs from resort status is, of course, the presence of a chair-lift system (the starting point of the walk), which may be of use to the summer walker as well as the winter sports enthusiasts. This route in fact makes use of the chair-lift to gain height above some beautiful Alpine pastures, a total rise of around 700m (2,300ft), with around 800m (2,600ft) of height gain to go on foot.

The chair-lift station is well signed from the centre of Mutters and there is ample car parking. However, unless you have two cars at your disposal, you will need to either park here and catch the train back down from Telfes, or conversely, park at Telfes and catch the train down to the start point. A single fare on the chair-lift was around £4 in 1989, and this gives you good value for money, as it is a long and quiet ride above the woods and meadows, which is split at half height at the Nockhof and terminates at the Mutterer Alm, a very typical *Alpengasthaus*.

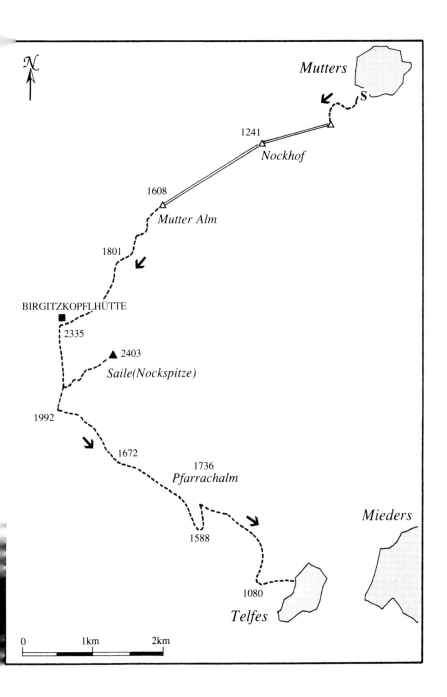

N

Mutters

S

1241
Nockhof

1608
Mutter Alm

1801

BIRGITZKOPFLHÜTTE
2335

▲ 2403
Saile(Nockspitze)

1992

1672

1736
Pfarrachalm

1588

Mieders

1080

Telfes

0   1km   2km

Forest track just outside Mutters

The first part of the actual walk follows the line of the ski tow and is in the same general direction as the line of lifts you have just ascended. This section of the route is quite steep and the ridge at the end of the tow system provides a welcome rest point, particularly since the small col bears visual delights in a number of directions. Just beyond here is the Pfriemeskopf. A short way past this point, the path splits – take the left branch, which then zigzags before climbing on to a fine ridge and junction with the path from the Raitiser Alm. A right turn here brings a steady ascent to the summit, at 2,403m (7,884ft) above sea level. Though this is not the highest, the steepest or most well known of the Stubai peaks, it possesses a stature beyond mere measurements – especially as it stands in a fairly isolated position at the eastern end of the Kalkogel mountain range. Some of its slopes are grassy, some craggy, but there is no real climbing as such – in many ways it reminded me of some of the higher Scottish peaks, but with the rough, red granite replaced by grey limestone. Probably the finest single virtue of the peak is the view. Being in an open position at the lower end of the valley, the panorama is eye-catching for a full 360 degrees. To the south is the col of Am Halsl, with the main Kalkogel peaks continuing beyond this. The Marchreisenspitze is the first high peak and just west of this the Malgrubenspitze and the Hochtennspitze can be seen, whilst further south again is the Schlicker Seespitze, the highest of these Dolomitic-looking peaks. To the west is Axamer Lizum and a small valley which descends gently to meet the main Inn valley, via the plateau on which Axams and Gotzens are perched. The view to the north is also first class. Beyond Innsbruck is the Karwendel, another area criss-crossed with paths and mountain huts. The initial barrier of peaks immediately to the north-west of the city, has many peaks of similar size, though I was rather surprised to see the Grosser Solstein at 2,541m (8,337ft), lower than the Kleiner Solstein at 2,637m (8,652ft)! However, it is the view from north-east round to south which is the most rewarding. Beyond the Brenner motorway, the Patscherkofel is prominent, with the Tuxer peaks beyond. Swinging further to the south, the impressive rocky buttresses which make up Serles are quite obvious, as is the ridge which runs in a southerly direction from that peak, via the Kesselspitze and the Ilmspitze, eventually on to the glaciers of Habicht.

On a good day, the summit is a great place to picnic – you will be able to spot people participating in parapente, and if you have a compass and map (which you should obviously have at all times), you can spend time identifying as many peaks as possible, from the hundreds which surround you. This is especially fine, when accompanied by traditional Austrian picnic fare, which inevitably includes – rightly or wrongly – the odd beer or two.

The descent from the summit is to the south-west initially, and eventually meets some zigzags which turn the route to the north-west for a short way, before meeting the path which traverses round from the Birgitzkopflhütte. (This can be reached in 20 minutes by turning right – north, at this junction rather than left – south). The way down from this junction firstly follows the path to the south to Halsl, a col at which half a dozen paths meet, and the main pass between the Stubai valley and the valleys to the north-west. Descend to the south-east from the col, ignoring a left turn which goes up to the Nederjoch, and continue descending the valley bottom to the point at 1,672m (5,486ft), where there is a three way split. The best route to follow here, is that which veers left and ascends gently to the Pfarrachalm (high meadow), though it is possible to follow the valley path direct to Fulpmes. Pfarrachalm is a superb place, perched at the edge of the great forests, which blanket the hillsides right down to the valley. It has some of the finest views available of the main floor of the Stubaital and of the Serles-Habicht ridge and it is a very special place to drink a well-earned beer. The final descent to Telfes is well marked and obvious, though the path which short cuts the road is steep and makes the valley feel even more welcome than it usually does.

Walk 6 Telfes – Kreith – Stockerhof – Telfes

Map no:	Kompass 1:25,000; Stubaital
Walking time:	3 hours
Grading:	E
Highest altitude:	1,156m (3,793ft)
Lowest altitude:	990m (3,250ft)

A delightful Panoramaweg type walk which is easy and suitable for a variety of ages and abilities. If wished, the steeper section up to the Stockerhof can be missed out by catching the train back to Telfes from Kreith. The bulk of the walk catches the sun from early morning until late afternoon, and being at the lower end of the valley, can benefit from good weather when the upper Stubai is sheathed in cloud.

The Walk

Either park close to the centre of Telfes itself, or at quieter times, limited parking is available at the start of the walk proper, where the metalled road finishes and the dirt road begins. The bus stops in Mieders, which is the closest stop, at around 15 minutes away. If you are travelling from the Innsbruck side, the train stops in Telfes, which is in fact as far as it goes. From the small station, continue following the most obvious, but ever diminishing roads, climbing slowly until just past the last of the houses the road surface deteriorates and gives rise to a few parking places. The dirt road which continues from here is the start of our route.

Already, some striking views of the upper part of the Stubai valley are revealed and the view down the meadows to Mieders is no less satisfying. The first ten minutes or so cover level ground, the terraced fields below dappled yellow, white and blue with flowers. No doubt there will be work going on here, for virtually every spare inch of this steep land is used for something. Grass is the main crop, valuable fodder for the long winter and everyone lends a hand, from the young man with the shiny new tractor to the old hand deliberately and accurately swinging a razor-edge scythe. This

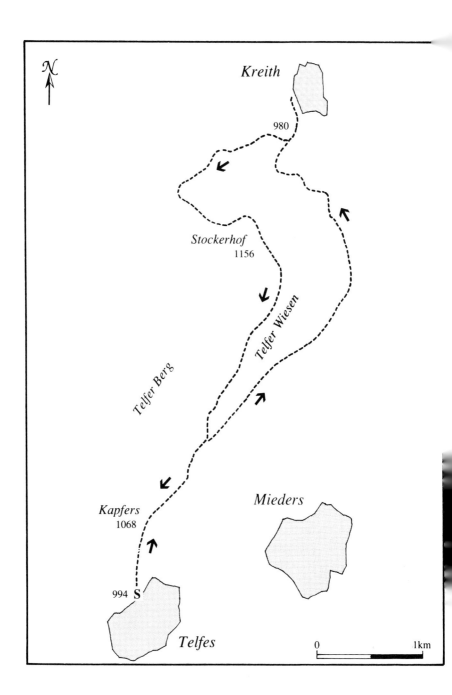

Kreith

980

Stockerhof
1156

Telfer Wiesen

Telfer Berg

Mieders

Kapfers
1068

994 **S**

Telfes

0   1km

latter method, along with the use of handrakes is very much in evidence as such a large percentage of the land on these valley sides is too steep for even the most versatile machine. On both sides of the path numerous old timber hay barns can be seen, full of character, gnarled and weathered like the tanned faces of the valley's older inhabitants. Here is a way of life which you can immediately sense is much closer to nature and the flow of the seasons than ours, where the small scale of the agriculture means a more intimate contact with the environment.

Continuing along, some impressive rows of avalanche-protection fencing can be seen high on the left – a reminder of the potential destruction which lurks high on so many Alpine hillsides in winter. Ahead, the Brenner motorway can be clearly seen, the only real eyesore here, although it is soon forgotten, compensated for by the backward view. The track gently descends for a while – it's ideal for cycling – and the railway comes into sight down to the right. Continue descending down a shady, tree-lined lane (you would be forgiven for thinking you were in the UK here), until the path crosses and recrosses the railway line. This section has some wonderful views over the Inn valley, and of the Karwendel mountains behind Innsbruck. Also visible is the huge bridge which forms part of the Brenner motorway – a view guaranteed to force nervous travellers on to the old road for any future descents into Innsbruck! At least you now know why you pay motorway tolls for this section.

Beyond here, a fascinating ironwork viaduct supports the railway across a small valley, around whose slopes the path contours, and it's a fine sight indeed to see the miniature train beetling across here, conjuring up images of an altogether more sedate and tranquil era. Soon the track rises gently to rejoin tarmac, at which point we take a left turn and follow a gently ascending track which leads up into the forest. This part of the walk is so typical of many of the forest tracks hereabouts, pleasant without being especially attractive, sustained without being arduous. Stockerhof is not too far away now and on a hot day you will no doubt be looking forward to partaking of its wide range of refreshments. It is very odd to reflect on how we would react in the UK to the scenario of high-level huts offering a wide range of refreshments, heavily waymarked paths and a very organised approach to walking in the mountains. Basically it just wouldn't happen, yet here it seems very right and proper, a quite normal and logical way of doing things.

Assuming adequate refreshment has been taken here, the way on lies across the field in front of the hut, where the path soon becomes unmistakable. Surprisingly, it ascends slightly in places, but soon begins a gentle descent through the forests, eventually rejoining the path we originally

Looking south up the Stubai valley from near Telfes

took from Telfes, just 10 minutes from our start point. In case you hadn't looked around on the way in, the village of Telfes is well worth spending some time in, having some superb murals and a very relaxed atmosphere.

The walk can be started from Kreith and done in reverse, or the train used to travel one way between the two stations, giving a number of variations. I also recommend this route for mountain biking and especially for photographers, as it has many features of interest as well as fine views.

Walk 7   Mieders – Fulpmes – Medraz – Kampl

Map no:	Kompass 1:25,000; Stubaital
Walking time:	1 hour 15 minutes
Grading:	E
Highest altitude:	1,000m (3,280ft)
Lowest altitude:	950m (3,120ft)

The Walk

This easy and enjoyable walk starts off in the village of Mieders which is only a short way from the Brenner Pass motorway junction. The Stubai bus stops in two places in the village and also at the chair-lift station, which is the first point at which this walk leaves the road. Mieders has some wonderful eighteenth century houses and a parish church built by the ubiquitous Franz de Paula Penz, a secular priest of nearby Telfes, so it is worth spending some time here before commencing the walk.

When you are ready, walk out of the village centre on the old road, which leads up to the chair-lift station. Take a left turn here, which leads up to the newer houses at Muhltal. At the first bend, the main track splits, and a subsidiary path splits off to the right into the forest. Carry on pleasantly enough through the woodland, crossing the Griesbach stream and descend to meet a good road – at which a right turn leads to the Café Jagerhausl (surely you're not needing refreshment already!) – while the route turns left along the Ebnersteig. If you want to visit the town of Fulpmes, you must go straight on at this point, down to the main road, across which the town centre lies. Fulpmes is the biggest place in the Stubai Valley, and as such does not have quite the character of Telfes or Mutters for example. It does have a rather interesting past however, once being a centre of the iron and steel industry with over fifty factories. It is still the home of one of the better known manufacturers of climbing hardware such as ice axes, crampons and pitons, not surprisingly known under the name Stubai. It is also interesting to note how well the factories are generally hidden by careful tree planting and good siting – their visual impact on the valley's scenery is really quite

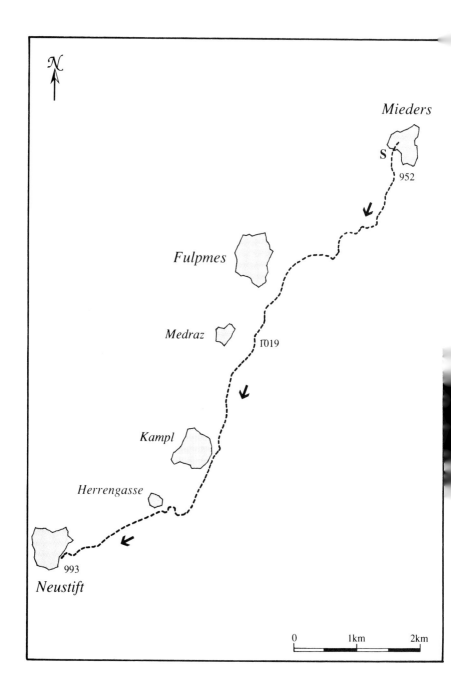

N

Mieders

S

952

Fulpmes

Medraz

T019

Kampl

Herrengasse

993

Neustift

0   1km   2km

Fulpmes, with the Elferspitze just to the right of the church tower

minimal. Fulpmes also has excellent sports facilities and is much more of a family resort than most other places hereabouts.

Returning to the Ebnersteig path, you can soon find an example of a sports facility which most walkers will want to avoid at all costs – the ski-jump! This is situated just a short way along this path and just before Medrazer Stille. Ski-jumping has evolved into a very specialized business, which has often been enjoyed on winter sports programmes. Ski-jumpers use very wide skis compared to their downhill counterparts, to give maximum glide and distance in the air, and the bindings are hinged at the toe, so the heel can lift. It is well worth standing at the top of or above one of these jumps; it is a humbling experience, as they are intimidating places where skill and nerve are tested to the full.

Above the highest rows of houses at Medrazer Stille, follow a road up to the left, then a path through the forest on the right which contours along to meet a clearing of meadows surrounded by woodland at Rastbichl. At the far end of this clearing, it is possible to drop down into Kampl, crossing the Hahlebach just before entering the village. Down on the main road, a short journey on the Stubai bus leads back down to Mieders. Alternatively, it is possible to continue the walk up to Neustift, a desirable option in my point of view. To do this, carry on contouring around the very upper edge of village and follow a track which skirts along the perimeter of the woodland and subsequently joins the good road/track which descends from the Pinnis valley. Turn right here, then left and enjoy a gentle descent past Obergasses and under the cable-car wires down into Neustift, which is reached by a path through the camp site. This last section of path provides a good view of the landing site for the paragliders, and commands some fine and open views. If you've got a picnic with you, this is probably the place to have it.

There are many more possibilities from here. The bus, or a pre-arranged lift will provide the easiest option to return to Mieders, but a series of paths can also be followed down the opposite side of the valley to that which you have just ascended. This is really the great beauty of this part of the valley – you can wander until you feel like a rest and then be faced only with most acceptable options – picnic, bar, *Gasthof*, bus ride.

My personal recommendation is to take a lazy day over this walk and make up excellent and entirely valid excuses for excessive eating and drinking along the way. Just enjoy the day out and don't eat too many portions of *Leberknodlsuppe*!

Walk 8   Mieders – Koppeneck – Ochsenhütte – Gleinser Hof – Mieders

Map no:	Kompass 1:25,000; Stubaital
Walking time:	3 to 4 hours 30 minutes
Grading:	M
Highest altitude:	1,625m (5,330ft)
Lowest altitude:	950m (3,120ft)

A fairly long, but easy walk especially if the chair-lift is used for the initial ascent.

The Walk

The chair-lift station just above Mieders is the starting point. The Stubai bus stops just down the road from the station on the edge of the village and there is ample car parking. The day starts with the usual choice – do you take advantage of the chair-lift or do you tackle the initial 700m (2,300ft) of ascent on foot? If you decide to walk, start by coming out of the chair-lift car park and turning up to the left past the Pension Alpenheim. Views back down to the village and to Serles open up very quickly, and the tarmac road soon deteriorates into a forest track. After a short way, the track splits and you follow the left fork which leads gently upwards, passing an excellent viewpoint and picnic table after about 20 minutes. Continue up a long series of forest trails, following signs for Sonnenstein. Here the uniformity of the solid stands of tall conifers is broken occasionally by firebreaks which open up marvellous views of the valley. Proceed to a junction at which the right turn is signed 'Sonnenstein', whilst straight on is marked to the 'Gasthof Koppeneck'. Follow the latter, which gently rises and leads to a well-placed rest point equipped with picnic table and seats. Turn right here, following the sign for Koppeneck, soon passing a newly painted (1989) shrine – typical of many to be found on paths in this area.

By this time on my ascent, the midday heat and the hard, dusty forest road were taking their toll but the terrain suddenly starts to open out above

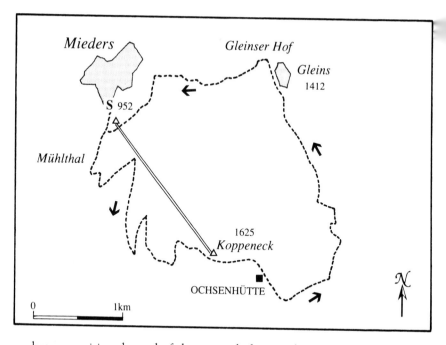

here, promising the end of the ascent before too long. At a conspicuous fork, a sharp left turn is taken which traces a line up through an open pasture area, complete with a herd of cows which were even more curious than usual – so much so that my pace involuntarily quickened as I recalled the damage I had seen similar beasts wreaking on a car earlier in the week. Fortunately, they soon became bored with me and I reached a small wooden hut, part of the winter sports scene here. At this point, you can either continue along the main path which passes under the chair-lift and leads to the Koppeneck in a long circular route, or cut up the cleared area above the hut in a more direct line which soon gives way to a large open area where the chair-lift finishes. It's immediately noticeable that the chair-lift, which is very close now is exceptionally quiet, lacking the conspicuous loud hum which so many of them possess. These high meadows provide plenty of good places to picnic and sunbathe and the views are tremendous – down into the Inn Valley and at the beige coloured peaks of the Karwendel beyond, directly across the Stubai valley to the great ring of Dolomitic-looking peaks above Fulpmes and back to Serles, the closest of the bigger mountains.

Also on this plateau is the Restaurant Koppeneck, a strange building which somehow combines modern styling with a more traditional look – never an easy thing to do. All the usual refreshments are of course available.

Restaurant Koppeneck, with the Kalkogel peaks behind

The route continues from the rear of the chair-lift drop-off and the Koppeneck by descending a steep, well-marked path through the woods, signed to the 'Ochsenhütte'. On reaching the main track, you will find it forks immediately, take the right fork and follow it to the hut, where you will probably find the usual complement of jolly, beer-drinking types soaking up sun and liquid in varying proportions. A gentle forest track ensues, rising steadily through fine specimens of fir and spruce and opening periodically to reveal the rocky buttresses of Serles. A long and placid descent then follows, (with fine splashes of Alpine butterwort on the path edge in places) and eventually a small track can be found leading off to the left which is signed 'Gleinser Hof'. This path re-crosses the main track and continues descending, leading to a gate which gives access to a long terrace, dotted with conspicuous yellow seats – one of the few examples of countryside furniture which didn't really gel with the character of the area. This track in turn leads on to a metalled road, where the views open up again and the Gleinser Hof is only a short distance away. A good time to arrive here is mid afternoon, when the sun is directly on this hillside and the cool drinks taste even better.

To the rear of the Gasthof is a very steep path leading down through the hay pastures, keeping to the right of a barn and then descending into the dark forest below. Keep to the left at the first prominent junction and then descend a very steep path between the trees to rejoin a good track. Go straight over this and continue down another steep section to yet another good track. Turn left here, go round a hairpin bend and then cut down to the left on any one of a variety of tracks which lead down on to a metalled road which drops down into the village. Turn left at an old barn with a conspicuous concrete chimney next to it (signed to the lift) and follow the obvious route back to the car-park. This last section sounds complex, but like many descents it is actually very obvious once you are on it.

Although this walk is not particularly strenuous, I found it very satisfying, especially as there are long sections of terrace which give excellent panoramas. It is highly recommended for family groups with youngsters who are capable of walking this distance and for anyone who requires a relaxing day amidst beautiful scenery. Much of the route would also be very suited to mountain biking and its finish could be extended to include a more appropriate descent by continuing past the Gleinser Hof and following long zigzag roads into the valley.

Walk 9 Fulpmes – Kreuzjoch – Sennjoch – Hoher Burgstall – Schlicker Alm – Fulpmes

Map no:	Kompass 1:25,000; Stubaital
Walking time:	4 to 5 hours
Grading:	D
Highest altitude:	2,611m (8,566ft)
Lowest altitude:	950m (3,120ft)

A reasonably long walk which takes in some steep ground, a little scrambling and some very loose scree. Good boots are advisable for this walk because of the nature of the terrain.

The Walk

The day starts with a slow, relaxing and very welcome ascent via the chair-lifts which go right up to 2,130m (7,000ft). Although this means of ascent can be avoided by those with stout legs, most walkers will take advantage of the lifts and enjoy the rest of the walk without the extra effort of ascending the first 1,200m (3,900ft) on foot. The chair-lift is in two sections, the first being steep but short, the second considerably longer and presenting very fine views indeed. The end of the lift system is at Kreuzjoch, where a restaurant complete with panoramic viewing windows attends to the tourists. The views from hereabouts are heart-stopping, the cirque of rocky peaks across to the right forming an awe-inspiring barrier of huge pinnacles and vertical faces, an uplifting sight which lightens packs and puts the spring back into weary legs.

From here, a good path contours round under the avalanche barriers, then zigzags steeply to a final ridge and the Sennjoch, just before which a shallow col gives good views to both sides of the ridge. Continue above the ski-lift stations here along a ridge which flattens off and gives access to a steeper ridge. The path zigzags steadily up here and then traverses under the left-hand side of the rocky lump of Niedrer Burgstall, passing a small cave which acts as a good landmark. At the end of the traverse, more steep zigzags

57

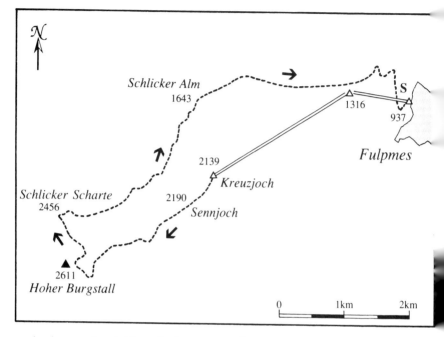

lead on to a level ridge, which gives a good viewpoint and rest place. Turning right here, will take you back up to this subsidiary summit if you have the time and inclination, otherwise it's a question of continuing along the ridge to the foot of a steeper section and a choice of turning left or right at the sign. The bulky rock summit of the Hoher Burgstall is directly above now, and it is reached by an easy route which avoids the sheer crags on this side. Take the left turn and then follow a path which scrambles steeply up past the big iron avalanche stoppers. The summit is close now, only some loose scree and easy scrambling remains before the summit ridge and cross is attained. The views are stunning and the position quite superb for a peak climbed so easily, though the faint-hearted or vertigo sufferers would do well to keep away from the eastern flanks of the peak. Most prominent from here is the Schlicker Seespitze, whose majestic south face possesses almost tangible scale and steepness, and the ring of peaks towering above grey screes and scrubby pine presents as fine a craggy outlook as anywhere in the region.

The descent involves retracing steps for a short distance, then veering right (the opposite side to the ascent) down a steep section of scree and ensuing zigzags which leads back down to the end of the flat ridge you left earlier, to climb to the summit. Though this descent is not particularly difficult, care should be taken on the loose scree, as limestone of this nature

The summit of Hoher Burgstall

is invariably slippery and more willing to move underfoot than any other rock type. Once down on the path, turn left and follow a long traverse whose continuation can be seen leading off towards a col from where another path (the eventual route) can be seen descending the shallow valley. The initial part of the traverse is level and some excellent picnic spots can be found. A good selection of plants can also be found here, typifying the species likely to be found more commonly on the limestone areas hereabouts: harebells, stonecrops, mountain valerian and saxifrages for example. As the traverse continues, it rises and falls increasingly, gaining height towards its end as it approaches the col, Schlicker Scharte. Above here towers the Schlicker Seespitze, a mountaineer-enticing summit if ever there was one, though most walkers would suffer palpitations at the thought of ascending its steep, exposed walls.

It's a long descent from here, though not at all difficult and the gradient is never severe. Impressive foreground crags and longer distance views, to the Marchreisenspitze and beyond, keep levels of interest high. At last, a road is reached. Cross this and continue descending through the forest down some steep paths which then rejoin the road which leads gently and easily to the Schlicker Alm. This is a popular ski centre in the winter months and caters for large numbers of people at all times of the year. A tiny old church just behind the Schlicker Alm is a popular visit and the area has a verdant and relaxing atmosphere, in direct contrast to the mountains we have just left behind. The descent from here is easy, following a good forest road all the way. The initial section is best avoided by following some paths through the woods on the left – as it is more comfortable on the feet and a delight to walk in. Lower down, the easy forest track continues its steady descent. It offers occasional glimpses of Serles on the other side of the main valley, and the views back up to the ring of mountains above the Schlicker Alm is absolutely superb. The tracks eventually lead back to the chair-lift station and a chance to review what will have been a memorable day out. It's worth remembering that the descent from the Hoher Burgstall involves a height loss of 1,674m (5,492ft) – a long way in anyone's books. Good footwear is essential to avoid discomfort and increase safety and on this walk I used a pair of Gronell Sympatex lined boots which proved to be the ultimate in comfort.

The lower section of this walk is popular in its own right and possible variations would be to descend from the chair-lift station direct to the Schlicker Alm, or to walk up to here from valley level, which is not a daunting task and gives some great scenery. The road up would also be excellent for mountain bikes.

Walk 10   Neustift – Milders – Seduck – Neustift

Map no:	Kompass 1:25,000; Stubaital
Walking time:	2 hours 30 minutes
Grading:	D
Highest altitude:	1,472m (4,829ft)
Lowest altitude:	995m (3,264ft)

A good evening walk that is not difficult and always on or very close to roads.

The Walk

The start of this route is Neustift, the main resort of the Stubai Valley and one which remains relatively unspoilt despite this. Its population is just over 3,000 and it can accommodate up to 6,500 visitors in a wide variety of categories from farmhouse to luxury hotel. It is 993m (3,258ft) above sea level, just about 15m (50ft) higher than the summit of Scafell Pike, England's highest mountain. Neustift was the home of Franz Senn, the priest who was a pioneer of mountaineering and of mountain-hut construction (see if you can spot the mural of him on this route), and the village has one of the finest churches in the area which also has the dubious honour of my prize for the most irritating bells anywhere – they will ring without apparent reason at virtually any time of the day or night and specialize in waking everyone up at around 5a.m.

The walk starts easily by following the main road to Milders out of the top end of the village (this is the one which passes the bulk of the shops). You will pass the Haus Franz Senn and further on the impressive Alpenhotel Fernau, where there are good views up towards the mouth of the glaciers – in summer dirty grey/blue ice pockmarked with stone and rubble and periodically peppered with icefall. Beyond here and just before the Chalet Tirol and the start of Milders village, a small path leads off to the right – remember this, as it is the path you will be returning on. Continue into the village and take a metalled road which bears rightwards, past neat, attractive

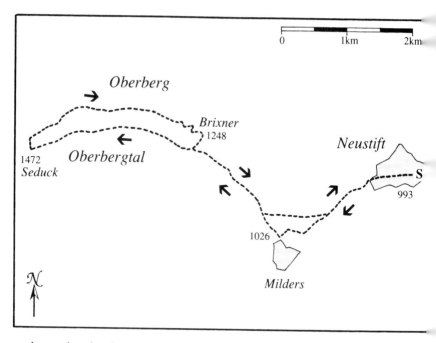

houses laced with troughs and baskets crammed with bright geraniums. There are no gardens as such here – all available land being used for hay, no matter how small – and so all the colour (and there's plenty of it!) comes from the window-boxes which liberally cover the fronts of most of these traditionally built Tyrol houses.

This road leads round to the rear of the Hotel Almhof, where a right turn (signed 'Franz Senn Hütte') marks the start of the ascent up the valley. The road rises steadily, but never steeply and you will soon reach a slightly flatter area where a track leads off to the right, following the river and running parallel to the road. There are lots of delightful places to stop here, and picnic places *par excellence* abound. The path rejoins the road at a point where it recrosses the river, and you follow a path which leads up its left bank to bring you out at another bridge and the Gasthaus Bärenbad. The remainder of the route to Seduck follows the road, the valley gradually opening out as height is gained. You will notice extensive riverbank stabilisation here, an essential requirement in many high Alpine valleys where water levels rise rapidly and the resulting destruction can be violent and awesome. Evidence of this can be seen about half-way up this part of the road, where a large section has been washed away. It was particularly impressive to note that in the space of a day, the repairs had been made, the

Looking down the Oberbergbach valley

road resurfaced, and only the tell-tale rubble above and below the wash-out point and the newness of the work remained as evidence of what had happened.

Seduck is situated a short way up to the right, along with a cluster of other buildings. You are now at 1,472m (4,829ft) above sea level – a height gain from Neustift of 479m (1,572ft), though it doesn't feel that much. If you want to extend the walk further up the valley, the Oberisshütte is about the same distance again as that from Milders to your present position, and is mostly on the road, though the final section from Stöcklenalm can be walked along the riverside.

The route back down the valley starts by crossing the river, passing Seduck on its right and following a path which traces a terrace-like line along the foot of the steep hillside, passing frequent farmsteads and huts such as Kuizen, Bucher and Salcher. This was for me the most interesting part of the walk. Not only are the views excellent, but there is a real human element to this section. There is a deeply rooted history of tradition here, with the first settlements going back to 1500 BC, and in more recent times, the mountain people's love of festivities, traditional costumes and warm hospitality has not been eroded by the commercialism which has cast a bland and characterless face on many other areas. You get the feeling here that they have not and will not yield to modern, commercial pressures – and that's a good thing. Indeed, it is well worth walking this part of the route slowly, giving your imagination time to get to work – you can dream a little, about the pastoral image of being a herdsman, which for many Alpine farmers is an image that still holds true.

The final part of this section leads on to a minor road which descends on to the main valley road at Bärenbad. From here, we can walk back down the road, passing a turn on the left which leads up to the Starkenburger Hütte, until just before you get back into Milders, a path leads off to the left (opposite a small road which comes in from the right). This crosses the river and drifts down to rejoin the main road from Milders to Neustift which you walked this morning. Don't expect high mountain views from this walk, or challenging paths which tread precipitous ground. Approach things in a different manner, look near rather than far, at buildings and flowers rather than distant peaks and you'll discover yet another facet to life in the Stubai Valley.

Walk 11   Neustift – Berg-Agrar – Elferhütte – Elferspitze – Pinnisalm – Issenanger Alm – Neustift

Map no:	Kompass 1:25,000; Stubaital
Walking time:	5 hours 30 minutes to 7 hours 30 minutes (depending on whether you use the chair-lift)
Grading:	C
Highest altitude:	2,505m (8,218ft)
Lowest altitude:	995m (3,264ft)

The route described will present no problems for fit and active walkers in good conditions, but bear in mind that early in the season there is likely to be plenty of old snow and when the route is difficult to follow, signs at the chair-lift station at Neustift (the starting point) will indicate this. There are also extensive areas of rocky terrain and care must be exercised at all times, especially on the later stages of the route. This is an extremely busy area and early morning or late evening ascents are advised during peak periods. All the paths are well marked and easy to follow, and the chair-lift runs from 3 June to 29 October.

The Walk

There is a vast difference between what walkers accept as walking and what climbers refer to as climbing. In between these definitions is an area of transition – a range of difficulties through which some walkers will pass successfully to discover the new thrills at the climbing end of the spectrum, whilst others will not wish to take the first probing steps into this transitional zone. In between, many walkers will start to tackle scrambling of different standards – British classics such as Striding Edge, Crib Goch and the Aonach Eagach ridge being well-known examples. But this is potentially dangerous ground to step in to, and at the upper end of this transitional zone, slight deterioration in conditions such as lower temperatures, wet rock or strong winds can tip the balance and push the levels of difficulty into the climbing

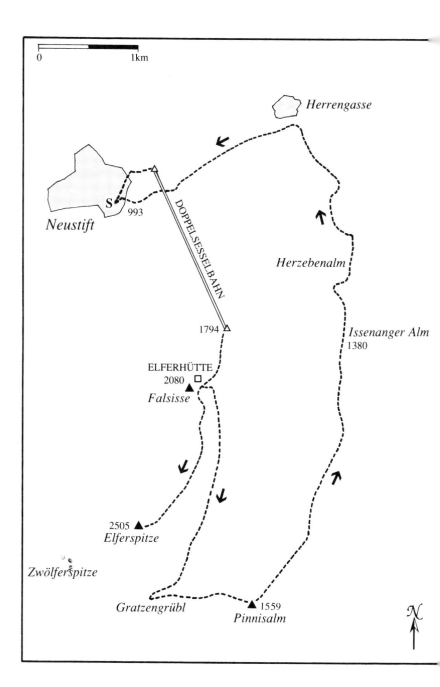

Herrengasse

Neustift

S 993

DOPPELSESSELBAHN

Herzebenalm

Issenanger Alm
1380

1794

ELFERHÜTTE
2080 ■
Falsisse

2505 ▲
Elferspitze

Zwölferspitze

Gratzengrübl

▲ 1559
Pinnisalm

0   1km

N

zone. Experience must therefore be built up gradually, preferably in the company of a more experienced companion, but the rewards, the opening up of new horizons and the discovery of new skills make the effort well worthwhile.

The ascent of the Elferspitze is an excellent choice of route at the lower end of this transitional zone. Most of the route involves walking and very easy scrambling, but in a climbing environment, and the only real difficulty is right where it should be – in the last few metres! As a final word of warning, a recent June visit revealed large quantities of old snow which obliterated much of the otherwise well-marked path, and blizzard conditions which gave something of the flavour of a Scottish winter ascent! If conditions turn out to be like this, your experience and common sense should dictate whether you continue, but otherwise, pick your day and the views and quality of the route will provide a memorable excursion.

There are two ways to start this route. Weak-willed (sensible?) walkers will take the new chair-lift out of Neustift which glides swiftly over the forests through which the alternative path zigzags. Using the chair-lift saves over 600m (1,900ft) of ascent, and provides plenty of amusement as it is designed for skiing and does not normally stop for access and dismounting! The path which leads to the same place can easily be located from the map and provides a long and fairly arduous ascent.

Either route will place you at the chair-lift station, Berg-Agrar. A steep path zigzags up the ridge from here to the Elferhütte (signed and easy to follow), where a typically wide selection of food and drink is available. A short way above the hut, the path splits, our route taking the right fork, which leads up on to the right side of the prominent ridge which runs down from the pinnacled summit area. After about half an hour the path splits again, the right fork giving access to the climbing routes here and in particular the very popular Nordwandroute, whilst we follow the left fork which continues fairly easily towards the start of the mountain proper.

From now on, we gradually enter a world of pinnacles, gullys, screes and crags, all the time secure in the knowledge that the path is generously waymarked. The views start to become exceptionally fine – to the left the complex and seemingly impregnable faces of the Ilmspitze, and to the right the main valley, which is by contrast flat, neat and welcoming. The views are further enhanced by the foregrounds of increasingly high rock towers and the sudden revelations of changing views through the tops of gullys and chimneys. Throughout this section the walking is not difficult, but the feel of the place – its atmosphere – gives the illusion that you are on an altogether higher and more dramatic mountain.

The Ilmspitze and the Pinnis valley from the Panoramaweg

Haymaking, Stubai style

Pinnisalm

Typically, there are a number of places where false summits can create some disillusionment, but on a walk such as this, maybe it's actually a pleasure to discover that you're not quite there yet! It will be obvious, however when the true summit is reached. Topped by a cross, it can only be reached by the ascent of a short chimney. Though only a few metres high, this is technically the most difficult part of the route, and the extra exposure (sense of height) experienced in the summit area gives it a bigger feel. Fortunately, the holds are big and some energetic squirming leads to the walker's high spot – a regal vantage point in a climber's world of soaring, blocky pinnacles and sheer crags. This is a taste of what can be achieved – maybe it will inspire you to higher things…?

The descent involves a retracing of steps back towards the Elferhütte. Go back past the junction with the path to the climbs, then back down to the junction above the Elferhütte. Turn right here and follow a long traverse which is clearly signed to Karalm. This traverse has superb views across on to the screes and faces of the Ilmspitze and it is possible to either take the turn to Pinnisalm, or to follow it in its entirety to Karalm, which adds on about one hour to the overall time. Either route leads down into the great valley, where in wet weather spectacular waterfalls rumble down into the river, and at any time, the massive grey screes are bound to impress. The Pinnisalm is a convenient refreshment point and prices are not unreasonable for a mountain café. The good track continues down the valley and through the forest, giving pleasant walking in a relaxing mood – a good wind down which leads to the Issenanger Alm restaurant with yet more nourishment for the needy.

A gentle but lengthy descent on a dusty road then leads back down to the main valley. To regain the start point, keep on the left of the river (on descent) and just as some houses are reached, look for a little path on the left which cuts across on to a road. Proceed through a small farm, passing under a raised walkway into a barn, and continue along the road past some delightful old barns until the path descends under the chair-lift to meet a bridge. It then leads across into a caravan site and out on to the main road. The chair-lift car park is only a couple of minutes down from here if required.

Other variations on this walk are quite possible and the combination of well-marked paths and easy-to-read maps (which are available virtually everywhere), means that it is quite possible to pick, for example, a shorter route down. The tobogganing track (the longest in Austria) from the chair-lift top down to Issenanger Alm is one such possibility, which then leaves the exploration of the Pinnisalm area for another day.

Whichever descent is chosen, it will be a pleasant and relaxing contrast to the rocky towers of the Elferspitze, but there is little doubt in my mind which part of the walk will have a permanent place in my memories. And who knows, perhaps one day you'll return and take the right fork – the one which leads to the Nordwandroute!

Walk 12   Neustift – Elferhütte – Neustift

Map no:	Kompass 1:25,000; Stubaital
Walking time:	2 hours 30 minutes to 4 hours (depending on the route taken)
Grading:	E/M
Highest altitude:	2,080m (6,824ft)
Lowest altitude:	995m (3,264ft)

This walk provides superb views, an excellent insight into paragliding and an easy way of enjoying some fine, high-level mountain views, if the chair-lift is used for the ascent. There is a chair-lift station in Neustift, and plenty of parking is available.

The Walk

There are a number of possible variations on this theme, which is essentially the reaching of the Elferhütte and the enjoyment of the fine views and situation. The easiest option is to use the chair for both the ascent and descent (Bergfahrt and Talfahrt), which in 1989 cost around £5 per person, with a small discount for having the Gastekarte, which also gives discounts at many other places. If this method is used, the actual walking time is considerably reduced, leaving a 35-minute walk up to the Elferhütte and a 25-minute walk back down. The alternatives are to use the chair for either ascent or descent (ascent recommended) or not to use it at all, in which cases the total times increase to those mentioned in the introduction.

If you take the first route you will ascend by the chair-lift and walk down. The fun begins right at the start of the day, with a chair-lift ride which is enlivened by the fact that it is designed for skiers to use. Wearing their skis, they are picked up by the moving chair and then glide off at the top to start their next descent. Of course, on foot, this is more difficult and as it is usual for the chair to continue to operate in this fashion, it necessitates accurate positioning for the pick-up and nimble footwork for the dismount. Don't worry through, it's not as difficult as it looks and if there is any doubt as to the

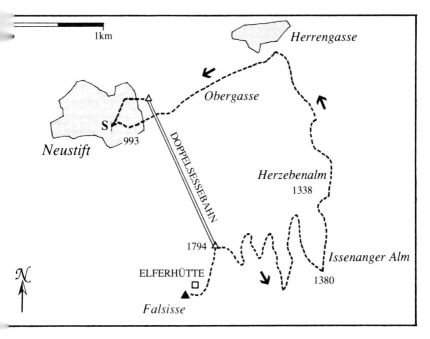

outcome, the controller will fortunately slow the chair down. The ride up is quiet and offers increasingly fine views. It also makes you glad you opted for this mode of transport, as you glide smoothly over the forest, occasionally glimpsing walkers ponderously ascending the winding tracks.

Assuming the dismount has left you in a fit condition to continue the walk, the way to the Elferhütte is very well marked and in good condition. It is an exceptionally popular walk, so be prepared to share the views with others – only very early or late season will see a quiet time. The path in fact ascends very steep ground, but it is well zigzagged, lowering the overall gradient and making the walk quite easy. On my last visit I even saw mountain bikers attempting the final section before the hut, throwing themselves enthusiastically upwards for a few metres before inevitably succumbing to gravity or a rock step. In fact, an old couple strolled gently past them, although I think they would have had the last laugh on the descent.

The walk up to the Elferhütte will take half an hour or so, and the reward is a magnificent view back down the Stubai valley and across to the cirque of mountains above Fulpmes. All manner of drinks and food can be obtained here and though busy, there is plenty of room. At this height, even on a sunny day it can be cool, so a spare jumper or anorak is a very useful thing to have.

The Elferhütte is also an ideal base for studying one of the fastest growing

The Elferhütte

sports in the Alps – paragliding or *parapente* as it is often known. You will probably already have spotted these colourful parachutes drifting lazily down from a variety of launch sites, but here is your chance to observe things first hand as the pilots commit themselves to the skies. Pilots are easily identified – they will normally have colourful clothing, padded paragliding boots and the real giveaway, the bulky rucksack into which the canopy has been carefully packed. (They may also have distinctive expressions, ranging from sheer terror to complete delight).

Assuming there is not much wind, the launching method used is the same for all the pilots. The canopy is removed from the rucksack and carefully laid out on the ground, the lines running down the hill. The leading edge of the canopy can be clearly identified as it has a number of holes in its front. This will be laid out so that it forms the up-slope edge of the canopy. The pilot will put on his special harness, a helmet, psych him or herself up and clip the lines of the canopy on to the shoulders of the harness. A final check and it's commitment time, which involves pulling the canopy forward at the same time as running down the hill as fast as possible. The snatch, and the forward speed of the pilot fills each of the holes that lead into the canopy with air, this air cannot escape, and immediately forms a semi-rigid wing which will eventually be weight-bearing. At around 22.5kph (15mph), the canopy will

Paragliding high above the valley

be wanting to fly, and a little application of the brakes will give the first lift. Assuming this is successful, the pilot will now be airborne and will be using a combination of body weight distribution and brake application to steer the canopy. In moments, they are a long way off, soaring effortlessly over the forests and looking for thermals which will give them lift and prolong the flight. Eventually, they all come down to land at a designated site close to the chair-lift station, where they can once again pack up their canopies and hop on to the lift, excited at the prospect of another flight. It looks amazing and feels even better. Just in case you're tempted, there's a paragliding school just outside Neustift…

It's easy to spend a lot of time here close to the hut, watching the flyers and admiring the view, but assuming you're walking down, the route firstly retraces its steps back to just above the lift station and then follows a well-signed and long forest road down to the right (on descent) into the Pinnisbach valley and the Issenanger Alm. In winter, this track forms the longest tobogganing run in the area, about 7km (4.5 miles), and it also gives a good method of ascent for mountain bikes. The Issenanger Alm is another very pleasant place to stop for refreshment. The terrace gets plenty of afternoon sunshine, food and drink is not particularly expensive, and the pond just in front is packed with trout, no doubt waiting to take their place on one of the restaurant's tables. A drink here is pretty much a must as the descent will probably have been dusty and hot, perhaps setting the tone for the day; lazy rather than energetic, watching rather than doing. The final descent from here is easy, but longer than you might think and the last section back to the car park is described in Walk 11.

It is possible to reverse this walk in its entirety, finishing by taking the chair-lift down, but this involves a gentle but long and dusty ascent and the former way is definitely recommended. There is one other way of descent of course, which is much easier, quicker and infinitely more pleasurable if you have a head for heights. Anyone for paragliding…?

Walk 13   Oberisshütte – Franz Senn Hütte

Map no:	Kompass 1:25,000; Stubaital
Walking time:	3 hours
Grading:	E/M
Highest altitude:	2,149m (7,050ft)
Lowest altitude:	1,742m (5,715ft)

This is a very popular hut which provides a high mountain setting along with relatively easy access. Many other walks radiate from here and it provides a good base for these, as well as a popular stopover for hut to hut walks. The paths leading up to the Franz Senn Hütte are generally in good condition, not too steep and ideal for a family day out, though it would not be recommended for small children. There are parking areas at or close to the Oberisshütte.

The Walk

From Milders, drive up the long valley, past Bärenbad, Seduck and Stöcklenalm (watch out for a vicious dip in the road past Seduck). Eventually, a small parking area is reached on the left of the road, just before a final group of buildings. Park here, or a little further on at the Oberisshütte itself, where a small charge is normally made. **Note!** There are numerous small parking areas on the roadside all the way up to the Oberisshütte, but be warned – if there are any cows about, park elsewhere. We saw one very smart Lancia reduced to scrapyard material by a small group of innocent looking Alpine cows.

If you start this walk in the afternoon, you are likely to be greeted at the outset by the sounds of jovial singing from the balconies of the Oberisshütte – one aspect of Austrian walking which is very different from other nationalities. Not for them the quiet search for seclusion. Beer and wine flow freely, voices ring out from the balconies of the huts – this somehow fits well with the overall atmosphere of the place. My advice is to leave here smartly, avoiding temptation and leave the celebrating until the walk is finished!

The hut and its surrounding building provide an interesting look at what

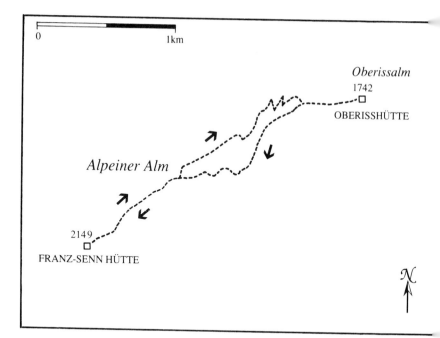

Oberissalm
1742
□
OBERISSHÜTTE

Alpeiner Alm

2149
□
FRANZ-SENN HÜTTE

0   1km

𝒩

can be achieved when new buildings are designed on old looks. Architectural styles, sizes, shapes and materials blend to give a most pleasing result, one which is common in much of the area.

This upper valley is very beautiful, its enclosing walls are steep and glaciers and snowfields shimmer invitingly ahead. Our path is obvious, contouring the hillside to the right of the hut and leading, after 10 – 15 minutes of gentle walking, to a junction. Both paths lead to the Franz Senn Hütte, but you can ascend via the left-hand path and then descend the other way. So, keep left and pass through an old wooden gate. The vegetation here is luxuriant in the peak of the summer and a wide variety of butterflies and flowers can be seen. Although late spring is probably the best time for flora, the middle of summer is the best time for the butterflies, and in July and August the air is constantly alive with them.

The route continues to ascend a rocky section beneath the old cableway, which is used to serve the hut with goods, and to carry rucksacks up and down, releasing the owners from the encumberment of heavy loads, spiky crampons and ice axes which seem oddly out of place on these tourist-laden tracks. A gnarled wooden gate marks an easing of the angle of ascent and provides a welcome rest point whilst beyond here, a gentler area is reached with an old building across to the right and waterfalls ahead. The hut can soon be seen

The Franz Senn Hütte

and the descent path joined for the shared final ascent. A fine rocky gorge lies down to the left, filled in the afternoon with a thundering torrent of glacier water and finally, an old bridge spans the same waters and gives access to the last short ascent to the hut.

The Franz Senn Hütte is named after the famous pioneer and co-founder of the DAV (German Alpine Club). It is normally a bustling, busy place with visitors of all conceivable ages, types, sizes and nationalities. As in other huts of its type, food and drink is readily available at prices which are good considering its location. Judging by the large numbers of tubby, red-faced, good-humoured and talkative walkers pouring out of the doors as we approached, its facilities are very well used. It may well be quite difficult for some walkers to immediately come to terms with this noisy, gregarious approach to the outdoors, but it's surprising how quickly a person can accept it – and it does have its good points!

Beyond the hut is a massive, flat valley bottom, at whose end the land rises in a huge corrie wall, culminating in the peaks of the Wildes Hinterbergl, the Schrandele, the Schrankogel and the Ruderhofspitze. Below these summits, impressive glaciers and seemingly impenetrable walls of rock and moraine provide an impressive sight. If time is on your side, it is worth strolling up this valley bottom, leaving the crowds of the hut behind and spending a little time tuning into the scale and beauty of this wonderful place.

Eventually though, we must all descend and the recommended route is to retrace your steps back to the point at which the ascent path joined another which came in from the right. Follow this, easily at first and then down a long section of steep zigzags, which eventually join up with the ascent route at its very first junction.

Other variations are possible. One very popular route is to ascend to a small lake, the Rinnensee, a site which commands superb views and which is well worth the extra 2 hour return trip if you have the energy and time. From the hut, follow a path which leads up to the right, then back left, eventually zigzagging before the final stretch to the lake. This route is well marked and popular, though quite strenuous. Its main attraction lies in its extra height, which gives a different perspective on the surrounding peaks and glaciers, and the lake, which provides an excellent foreground.

Whichever route you take, I wonder if you'll be tempted to slip into the Oberisshütte when you get down? I know I was.

Walk 14   Oberisshütte – Franz Senn Hütte – Seduckalm – Seduck

Map no:	Kompass 1:25,000; Stubaital
Walking time:	4 hours 30 minutes
Grading:	M
Highest altitude:	2,249m (7,379ft)
Lowest altitude:	1,742m (5,715ft)

Although there are no real difficulties on this walk, the traverse from the Franz Senn Hütte is long and in some places loose, though the paths are often repaired quickly. It provides plenty of 'exposure' (a feeling of height), and has superb views. The route can be extended considerably if required (*see* Walk description).

The Walk

To reach the Oberisshütte you drive up the valley from Milders, as for Walk 13. As the walk finishes at a different point, lower down the valley, try to have a lift laid on to take you back to the Oberisshütte at the end of the walk. No public transport is available and walking or hitch-hiking are the only alternatives.

The first section of this route is the same as for Walk 13, involving a fairly leisurely stroll up to the Franz Senn Hütte. The second part of the walk on the traverse, which is its real attraction, is particularly pleasant early in the morning when it basks in the sun's first warm rays, and is normally without many other people. Therefore, it is advisable either to stay the night in the Franz Senn Hütte and depart early, or set off at first light from the valley. This sort of approach means that the bulk of the midday and afternoon heat is avoided for the initial climb out of the valley, and the traverse becomes particularly pleasant. One alternative to this for very hot weather is to make the walk an evening one. This means that the traverse will not attract any sun, but this may be compensated for by cool air and wonderful sunset colours.

The hut provides an excellent rest place and view point, and is likely to be

81

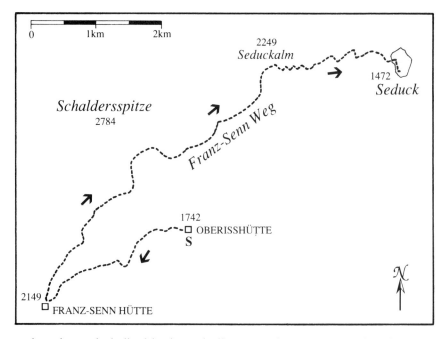

busy during the bulk of the day with all manner of mountain users, from long-distance hikers to extremely casual day-trippers. Our route crosses a bridge behind the hut, turns right and follows some very steep streamside zigzags to a junction, whose left fork is signed Rinnennieder, and whose right fork is signed Horntaler Joch. Follow this branch and cross a stream (a waterfall higher up). The narrow path then starts to traverse the hillside, ascending slightly at first and always with steep ground above and below. The views on this walk now start to become exceptional, the paths to the Franz Senn Hütte are map-like below and the peaks on the opposite side of the valley jut boldly against the skyline. Good eyes will pick out the long traversing path which leads from the Franz Senn Hütte into the Platzengrube, and then ascends to the col near the Basslerjoch, before descending into places well hidden from here.

The path crosses another stony stream and ignores a fork back up to the left as we come to an open, grassy area which gives a fine viewpoint and a most convenient picnic spot. The whole hillside along which this path traverses is a botanist's delight, being carpeted with a multi-coloured array of all manner of Alpine flowers, with buttercups, harebells, crowfoot, saxifrages and hogweeds vying with many others for their precarious space on these ever-changing slopes. Beyond here is a tiny rock step, complete with the

The Franz Senn Hütte and the valley beyond from the Franz Senn Weg

obligatory (and completely useless) iron holds. After this a long belvedere leads ahead, where broken cliffs above and below provide a real sense of space and exposure, whilst the path remains in good shape.

Quite suddenly, an enormous grassy bowl appears, the continuation of the path clearly visible as it contours around it. Access is guarded by another short rock step, yet again supplied with artificial holds and the path then starts its long loop round, hugging a contour which curls in a fine line around this steep bay. A couple of rocky streams fall across the route and these places especially give rise to a profusion of small plants, with many types of saxifrage and other wet-loving alpines such as butterwort and spiniest thistle. At the end of the bay is a final, land-slip prone stream and a short, steep section of zigzags, which is fortunately not nearly as bad as it appears from a distance. Stop and cast a glance backwards here, for the views of the upper part of the Alpeiner Bach and of the path you have just used are exceptional.

More fine traversing leads to another short, steep section, complete with decaying wire rope but it poses no problems. By now, the views ahead are becoming increasingly impressive, the distant limestone peaks of the Karwendel looking strikingly bright by comparison with the darker, rocky peaks to the rear. A short way further, a small hut, the Seduckalm is reached – the point at which the descent begins. Instead of following the main path, which continues its gentle ascent, cut down to the right past a flag, where the path down to the valley becomes increasingly obvious. It is grassy at first, but then it steepens and drops into the forests – a complete contrast to the gentler, wide and busy paths used earlier in the day. The descent is steep at times, and quite long, but the knowledge that every few feet brings the valley that much closer to hand is sufficient inspiration and the valley floor is soon reached. From here, either rendezvous with your pre-arranged lift, walk or hitch back up for your vehicle at the Oberisshütte, or continue to walk back down to Neustift via part of Walk 10.

This walk can be extended considerably for the leather-lunged, iron-thighed brigade by continuing the traverse from Seduckalm right through to the small lakes at Oberberger, just south west of the Schlicker Seespitze. From here, a descent to Neustift can be made by following the well-marked path past the Starkenburger Hütte. Although this is a mighty fine walk, it is long and arduous and adds another $2^1/_2$ – 3 hours on to the route. The way is obvious and not difficult, and there can be few finer places in the Stubai to relax with a well-earned drink than the Starkenburger Hütte if you have the energy and the time.

Walk 15 Volderau – Krossbach – Mischbach Waterfalls

Map no:	Kompass 1:25,000; Stubaital
Walking time:	2 hours
Grading:	E
Highest altitude:	1,400m (4,600ft)
Lowest altitude:	1,126m (3,694ft)

It is an easy and low-level walk which is especially suitable for family groups or for those with limited time.

The Walk

The starting point of this walk is the tiny hamlet of Volderau, which lies on the main Stubai valley road. The Stubai bus stops here and there is also a variety of limited parking.

There are two major waterfalls in the upper part of the Stubaital which are visible from the road. This walk revolves around the first of the two – a powerful and impressive fall which although lacking the width of its higher neighbour, compensates by virtue of its sheer ferocity.

Its main supply of water comes from the glaciers and feeder streams on the Schaufelspitze and Habicht, a formidable drainage area which provides colossal amounts of water during periods of heavy rain and thaw. In such conditions, the water can turn brown and grey – a filthy torrent which can revert to sparkling waters of great clarity overnight. The peak known as Habicht is the highest in the east Stubai and was once considered to be the highest mountain in the Tyrol! It was first ascended in 1836 by its ordinary route, which is little more than a high-level scramble in good conditions, and which is typical of the type of excellent introductory Alpine route which this area abounds with. It also boasts a north ridge and a north face, the latter considered to be the hardest ice climb in the region. For anyone contemplating making an ascent of the easy route, it starts from the Innsbrucker Hütte and takes approximately $2^1/_2$ – 3 hours to reach the summit.

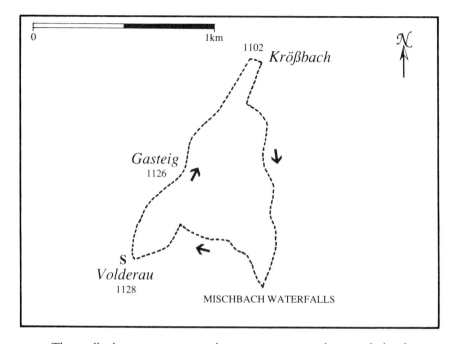

The walk, however, starts in less austere surroundings and the first landmark to look out for is the very obvious Hochstubai camping and caravan site. The route starts off by entering the campsite, crossing the river and following a path which leads to the right after the main building and descending slightly past the part of the site reserved for tents. The river on the right will be full of icy cold, grey glacier water – definitely not for swimming, and the waterfall which is the eventual target can be seen (and heard) ahead. Fifteen or twenty minutes of gentle strolling follows, along a flat track which is occasionally used by horse and traps to ferry sightseers along the valley. This is most definitely a place to take it easy and relax. The coniferous forests which clothe the valley side provide shelter from a hot midday sun and a variety of flowers colour their margins, contrasting with the dark and mysterious interior. As in most places here, these areas are too steep to walk in comfortably, so exploration is naturally discouraged.

The broad track finishes back at the road, and it is necessary to walk back along this to the point at which the path to the waterfall leads off. This point is reached fairly soon, and is well marked with the word 'Wasserfall'. This path is recent (1989) and rather unusually, has been constructed between fences and comes complete with artificial steps. A few minutes of rather more strenuous activity than has so far been found gives access to the base of the

One of the waterfalls

waterfall, and a noisy, though very beautiful picnic and relaxation site. A new bridge and reinforced banks have been constructed to control the flow of the water, a control whose necessity is all too obvious in most conditions.

It is easy to scramble down to the riverside at the base of the falls, where the power and scale can be appreciated at a distance which is neither too noisy nor too wet. It is also possible to scramble further up the river bed, but when the river is high, it may be impossible, and in any case you soon reach a point where further progress is denied to any but highly competent climbers. Beyond here, the ground is loose and potentially very dangerous – you have been warned!

Further exploration here is severely limited by the increasingly vertical nature of the terrain and the only way to go is down, following the new track which leads in a straight line to rejoin the road. A short walk back up the valley leads to the start point. There is a tiny 'locals bar' here which was recommended. Look out for it and pop in for a drink – it's very different – more than that I'm not saying!

The other big waterfall in the upper part of the valley which descends from Sulzegg is only a few minutes drive up the valley and is perfectly obvious from the road. Access to it is equally obvious. It's another impressive place and a pleasant half-hour can be spent loitering at its base. Being considerably wider than its neighbour, in conditions of spate it can be even more impressive and is the cause of much shutter clicking, pointing and squealing tyres. Both falls are not to be missed.

Walk 16 Falbeson – Neue Regensburger Hütte – Franz Senn Hütte

Map no:	Kompass 1:25,000; Stubaital
Walking time:	2 hours 30 minutes to 5 hours (depending on how much of the walk you cover)
Grading:	D
Highest altitude:	2,786m (9,140ft)
Lowest altitude:	1,150m (3,773ft)

This walk can be split into sections. However, it is easier to use the same route for the journey to and from Neue Regensburger Hütte and the time you need will total around 4^1/$_2$ hours.

The whole route as described covers some high and impressive mountain country and should not be undertaken lightly. You should watch out for snow early and late in the season and be prepared for rough scree.

The Walk

Due to the fact that the route starts and finishes in different valleys, you must first consider the logistics of transport. The local Stubai bus (ask for the Regensburger Hütte stop which is close to the café Knoflach in Falbeson), links the start point with the rest of the Stubai valley, but does not go up into the Oberiss valley where the route finishes. The descent of the latter can be undertaken by pre-arranged lift (the best option), the daily jeep service (enquire about availability beforehand), or by walking back to Milders, which is least recommended unless two days are being taken over the trip.

This is a really worthwhile walk to do, either as a single day excursion for the fast and fit, or as a two day tour for those wishing to travel at a more leisurely pace. To do the walk comfortably in a day means making an early start and maintaining a steady pace, whilst the two day trip can be done in two ways. Firstly, you can walk as far as the Neue Regensburger Hütte on the first day, perhaps also taking in the pretty Falbesoner See and complete the route to the Franz Senn Hütte and beyond on the second day. Alternatively,

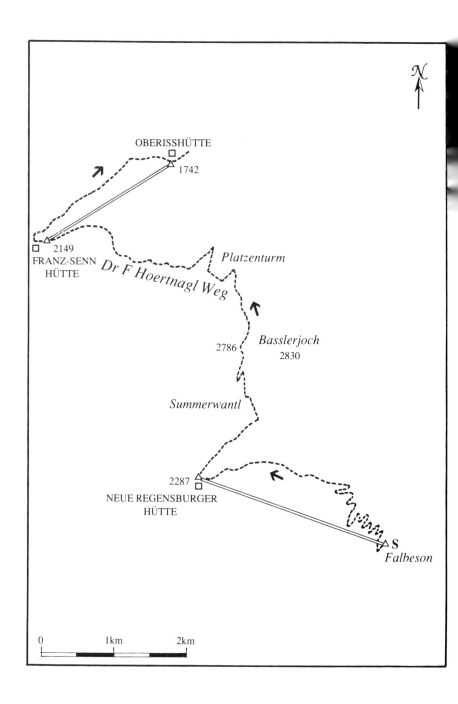

you can walk right over to the Franz Senn Hütte on the first day and enjoy a leisurely descent by Walks 13 or 14, possibly combined with the complete descent into Neustift via Walk 10. I recommend the former, though the final decision as always is in your own hands.

The first section of the route is tough going, especially on a hot morning, although the dark forest canopy can provide some welcome respite from the morning sun. From the Café Knoflach grind a way ponderously up very steep ground until you reach the upper limit of the forest and the Falbesoner Ochsenalm. It's around 620m (2,000ft) of ascent, but it feels more and a drinks stop is pretty much essential. This is a grand situation, the high valley being surrounded by impressive looking peaks and the forests dwindling, phasing out into rock and scree. The route to the Neue Regensburger Hütte continues on the north side of the river, more easily at first but then steepening uncomfortably for the final hundred metres. The hut is well sited on the rim of the valley and has free hot showers! It is also right on the edge of the Hohes Moos (High Moss) and is a really good start point for ascents of many of the surrounding peaks and for many one or two day trips.

If you are staying the night here, or if you are just up for a day trip, you should consider walking up to Falbeson Lake, or See, which is an hour or so's walk along path number 138, which leads eventually right round to the Dresdner Hütte. The path keeps to the right (north) of the river and crosses several tributaries which spill down from the snowfields high above, where several 3,000m (9,800ft) peaks are to be found. The See itself is in a high and barren area and it is likely to feel cold here when there is any wind about. Nonetheless, its remote setting makes it a fine point to linger in good conditions and if you've made an early start it is an excellent lunching point. Descent from here back to the hut is by the same route.

The way from the Neue Regensburger Hütte to the Franz Senn Hütte is for the most part well marked, but some sections in the scree are less obvious, and in snow and mist route finding can be quite tricky. The first section, the Windtratten, is a pleasant contour, and is a good warm up for the ascent to come. After about half an hour's walking, the path splits off to the left at a point just below the Summerwantl. (The continuation keeps on contouring to the Milderaunalm, from where Milders and Neustift can easily be reached.) This section of the walk is relentless, climbing 500m (1,600ft) up ever steepening ground to the Schrimmennieder, at 2,706m (8,878ft). The last section up to the col winds through a steep, rocky gully – hard work, but worth it at the top. From here, a short detour to the east leads on to the summit of the Basslerjoch – 2,330m (7,644ft). The fine views make the 15 minute walk well worth the little extra effort, with the Serles/Habicht ridge and the

The route down to the Franz Senn Hütte from the Schrimmennieder
The Schrimmennieder is the low point on the skyline and
the path descends across the screes below

Wilder Freiger glacier being particularly prominent.

From the col, which is little more than a knife edge ridge, descend in a north-easterly direction at first, making a descending contour down rough, scree-scarred terrain to reach some large zigzags at the Platzengrube. Below here, another section of zigzags brings you to a river crossing, where the path starts to contour more, across towards the Franz Senn Hütte. Another stream crossing and a contour around the ridge which falls several hundred metres from the Ostl. Knotenspitze brings the hut into view and starts a final easy contouring descent. The scale of the descent route has been truly impressive, the screes are extensive and, seen from across the valley, figures are easily lost in the vastness of this rocky wilderness.

The Franz Senn Hütte is owned by the Austrian Alpine Club and is a large, hotel-like place which imparts an atmosphere of jovial popularity due to its proximity to the road below. All that remains is to relax here and replenish your energy supplies, and to decide on the next move. If you are staying the night and descending the following day, I thoroughly recommend taking the route described in Walk 14, which consists of a fine contouring path, high above the valley with excellent views of the descent to the Franz Senn Hütte from the Schrimmennieder.

If you are descending immediately and want the quickest route, just follow the main path down to the Oberisshütte, which is well marked and normally heavily populated.

Walk 17   Grabaalm – Sulzegg

Map no:	Kompass 1:25,000; Stubaital
Walking time:	2 hours 30 minutes (return)
Grading:	E/M
Highest altitude:	1.750m (5,740ft)
Lowest altitude:	1,500m (5,000ft)

This is a popular walk – probably one of the most popular in the valley. It should be obvious therefore that at busy times the route should only be frequented by gregarious walkers who don't mind sharing the superb forests and mountains with hordes of other gregarious walkers. At quieter times of the year and during the early morning and evening it becomes a more reasonable proposition for those who require a short, easy walk without the crowds.

The Walk

The starting point is Grabaalm, a small cluster of buildings opposite a huge waterfall, a few kilometres down the valley from its end at Mutterbergalm.

The start point for a walk could not be more spectacular. A 200m (650ft) waterfall crashes and free falls its way down to the floor of the valley. It's an awesome sight, especially after heavy rain or thaw of higher snows and it is worth spending some time at its foot on a hot summer day, relaxing in the cool spray and soaking up (literally!) its powerful atmosphere. The start of the path is reached either by car (plenty of parking) or by the Stubai bus which stops a little way up the hill. Just upstream from the waterfalls, a track leads down to the river and a wooden bridge gives access to the paths on its south-east side. The foot of the waterfall can be reached by turning left, and the path which leads up to the Sulzegg is the right-hand branch.

A typical day here will see every conceivable type of walker imaginable. The sturdy, high mountain men will be starting off here to walk up to the Sulzenauhütte and beyond, to the high glaciers and the Zuckerhütl – the highest peak in the Stubai at 3,505m (11,499ft). (Its name means Sugarloaf,

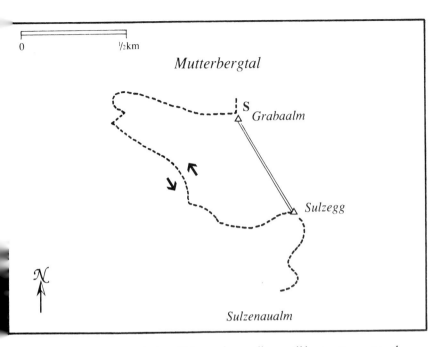

0   ½km

S
Grabaalm

Sulzegg

N

Sulzenaualm

a very appropriate translation.) Hut-to-hut walkers will be starting out to the same initial goal, then striking off to the Nürnburger or Dresdner Huts. There will also be the casual walkers. If nothing else, you certainly come across a wide variety of people here and in some ways, this adds to the holiday atmosphere in a not altogether disagreeable way.

The route starts gently enough, following the riverside upstream, meandering between lichen-draped larch and fir and threading a way amongst humps and hillocks of bilberry and fern. After a short distance, the path veers left into a long series of zigzags which weave upwards through the steep forestside. Some of these zigzags – the walking equivalent of a series of hairpin bends negotiating an otherwise undrivable hillside – are starting to wear as walkers cut off the corners, quickly eroding the fragile ground between. This is now a serious problem in many of the UK's more heavily used mountain areas and it is also starting to be seen more and more often in the Alps. In order to help the situation, it is important to keep to the zigzags and not to short cut, especially in descent. The forest floor, like a steep, poorly vegetated mountainside, is especially vulnerable to erosion from water and frost once walkers have scuffed away the frail upper surface, so please take care here.

The higher you get up this path, the less of a problem this becomes as the

The waterfalls at Grabaalm

ground gets progressively rockier and steeper, and there is little choice but to follow its exact line. This ascent is a little on the arduous side, but this is counteracted by the beauty of the forest through which it climbs. Sunlight filters gently through the canopy of green-grey conifers and it is unusually quiet for a woodland, the altitude and its make-up rendering it less attractive to wildlife than many of the mixed, lowland forests. Eventually, the path eases and continues a long, leftwards track which quite suddenly meets the river that feeds the big waterfall. And then equally suddenly, it bursts out into a wonderful high valley, pancake-bottomed and sealed with a precipitous headwall split on its left by a long waterfall. The valley floor contains a sparkling river, fed with melting snow and ice from higher regions and the overall setting is quite stunning. On the very rim of the headwall can be seen the daringly perched Sulzenauhütte, positioned so that it shouts out its challenge to all those who gaze up from this lower place.

Picnic places abound here for those who have carried their own food and there are huts to eat at for those who haven't, as well as cool beer, shade from a hot sun, warm drinks and shelter from a cool wind. This is a place to relax and savour, a magical mountain paradise from where retreat is reluctant, normally only enforced by time or a chill which descends once the afternoon sun disappears. If time and energy allow, the Sulzenauhütte is within reach, via a series of arduous zigzags which climb out of the right-hand side of the end of the valley. Allow $1 - 1^1/_2$ hours for this extension, with another hour for the descent. It is probably worth the extra effort for the view which this lofty perch provides.

The descent is a direct reversal of the ascent, right back to the foot of the waterfalls. An extension of the walk is possible here, by either walking up river to Mutterbergalm and the bus, or by walking downstream to catch the bus just down the valley from Schangelairalm. Either way will add on about an hour to the walk.

As a summary, this is an excellent family or off-day walk, which provides a number of extensions if required. Its only drawback is its popularity, but this can be overcome by careful planning.

Walk 18 Mutterbergalm – Dresdner Hütte
– Beiljoch – Sulzegg – Grabaalm

Map no:	Kompass 1:25,000; Stubaital
Walking time:	3 hours to 6 hours (depending on route)
Grading:	D
Highest altitude:	2,676m (8,779ft)
Lowest altitude:	1,721m (5,646ft)

This is a higher-level walk which is likely to have extensive snow cover early in the season and which could have snow in its upper sections at any time of year. An ice axe should be carried in these conditions and care taken in one or two places just past the col, where the path is steep.

It is best to do the section from the Dresdner Hütte onwards either very early or very late, as this gives most freedom from the crowds which are likely at both ends of the stage. Also, remember that the walk finishes at a different place to the start point and you must either arrange for a lift or catch the bus to avoid a long walk back up the valley.

The Walk

There are three ways to start this route, all of which go to the Dresdner Hütte and the choice depends on how much energy you have and how long you want your day to last. The simplest way is to catch the gondola up to the hut. (This is also by far the quickest way!) This does have an advantage if time is short as it enables the bulk of the walk to be undertaken in a total of just over 3 hours. A second alternative is to walk up the path from the rear of the gondola station. This is a fair way – a good hour's hard walking, but it is well zigzagged and the ascent is never very steep; however, its proximity to the gondola reduces its attraction. The third way is to follow Walk 20 via the Wilde Grube. This is by far the longest route to the hut, but it combines to make a really superb day's walk and is highly recommended.

Whichever route is followed, the Dresdner Hütte is the first objective. From here, the first section of the next part of the walk can be seen on the

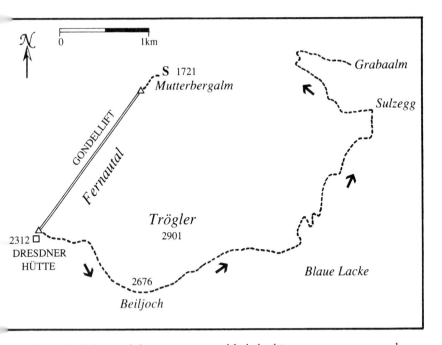

other side of the gondola station – an unlikely looking way, up a steep, rock-strewn hillside. Gain the path just behind the station and follow it over a narrow wooden bridge. Continue, rising steadily across a scree and rock slope to reach some zigzags, from where some excellent views are starting to open up, both of the glaciers and of the peaks on the north side of the main valley. After a short way, the path splits, the left fork leading to the more difficult Trögler, while this route continues up to the right, ascending, crossing and re-crossing a steep ridge. This section begins to provide a real mountain atmosphere, as you leave the hut and the gondola well behind and ascend a path which is always easy, but actually ascends some very steep and increasingly rocky ground. As height is gained, so the feeling of isolation increases and the ridge gradually eases, giving way to a huge area of rock and scree, the way now punctuated with cairns and the slabby rocks often set like steps, making the going considerably easier and reducing the chance of a twisted ankle in this unruly jumble of blocks.

Soon, a myriad of tall cairns are reached in a rocky col and the view across the next valley to the enormous glaciers beyond is breath-taking. This is a truly awesome place to be, a real and impressive change from the lift-encumbered views behind. The tall, narrow cairns and the desolation of the savage, ice-clad world ahead give a Himalayan feeling to the scene and in

The Sulzenauhütte – the descent path is across to the right

good weather there can be few finer places in the Stubai.

The descent from here is steep, and in snow-bound conditions, care should be exercised. This section soon eases and leads on to a ridge of moraine which gives good views down on to the tongue of the glacier. Follow the moraine on to a steep hillside, where a fortunately short ascent gives way to a long drift down into the main valley. There are a couple of interesting things to watch out for down here. Firstly, the Klettergarten – a climbing training area. Amazingly, the routes are delineated on the rock with broad stripes of paint, rather like a vertical version of the white lines down the middle of the road. This cannot be condoned anywhere, let alone here in this high mountain setting and it left me wondering if this was the same sport that I love so much. The second thing to notice is the natural environmental damage that has been caused by flooding, especially in the lower reaches of the valley. The scale of destruction in these Alpine regions can be amazing, and looking at the changes in this area it is easy to see how roads and bridges can be swept aside down in the valley.

The Sulzenauhütte is the next landmark. Perched on the rim of a huge rocky corrie, it is an impressive site indeed and an excellent place for a final rest before the next descent. Go left from the hut and follow a traversing path which then leads to a long series of stony zigzags which descend very steep ground to the flat bottom of a delightful high valley. Once down here, the audacity of the position of the Sulzenauhütte can be fully appreciated, as it can clearly be seen perched high above, with great crags below and a huge waterfall across to the left.

Down in this pancake-floored valley are a small group of huts – Sulzenaualm – which are very popular earlier in the day with the hordes who approach this place via the route which we now take as our descent. Follow the broad path which crosses a couple of bridges over the usual milky water and take a last glance back up the massive headwall before heading off down the long, traversing descent into the main valley. This leads on to some zigzags and eventually down to the riverside path. From here, your route will depend on your pick-up point, but the ideal is to continue down the riverside, to finish the day by the enormous, slabby waterfall which rushes down to the Grabaalm, where feet can be cooled and the evening's meal looked forward to with relish.

Walk 19 Mutterbergalm – Dresdner Hütte – Beiljoch – Sulzenauhütte – Nürnburger Hütte – Ranalt

Map no:	Kompass 1:25,000; Stubaital
Walking time:	5 hours 30 minutes
Grading:	D
Highest altitude:	2,676m (8,779ft)
Lowest altitude:	1,303m (4,275ft – finish point) 1,721m (5,646ft – start point)

The Walk

A great day's walking can be had on this route, but make sure you wait for good weather, as there are some excellent viewpoints and the main pass is quite high and descent from it would be unpleasant in snow. Although the recommended time is around $5^{1}/_{2}$ hours, a fast party would do it in 4 hours, but like all the walks in this book it is probably best to take a little longer and enjoy the superb scenery. Don't forget that it is also possible to combine a stay in the Nürnburger Hütte with this Walk – an option which I can recommend highly.

The day starts by taking the cable-car up to the Dresdner Hütte. However, it is possible to walk up to this point as in Walk 20, or by following the path which runs up to the right of the cableway. This adds on at least an hour and a half to the day and is not recommended unless an especially long day is required for some reason, or unless you have a particular aversion to the cable-car. A single ticket to the first station is only a couple of pounds or so and is well worth it from the point of view of energy conservation – yours that is!

From the busy Dresdner Hütte and its scarred environs it would be a pleasant prospect to look ahead to the ascent to the Beiljoch, were it not for the fact that it looks relentlessly and increasingly steep and unnervingly rocky. The path however lacks bite and in reality it presents little more than easy walking, though it is steep in places and is mostly on rock and scree. (A full description of the ascent to the col and of the descent to the Sulzenauhütte

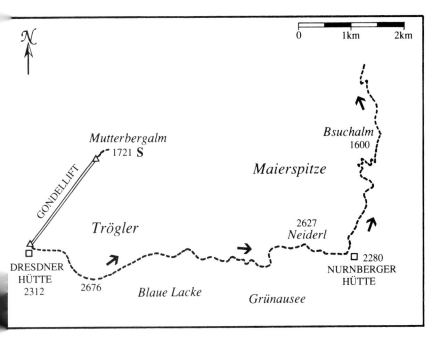

can be found in Walk 18.) There is a short variation possible on this ascent, which involves gaining the summit of the Grosser Trögler. About 20 minutes from the Dresdner Hütte the path splits and the left-hand branch is clearly signed to the Trögler. This will add on around an hour to the walk in total, but in many ways it is worth it as you will actually have reached a summit during the day, and one which has brilliant views to boot – the north side of the Zuckerhütl – Wilder Freiger group looking particularly enticing as their rocky ridges and summits struggle free of the all-embracing glaciers.

The latter option is slightly harder going than the original, and involves an extra 230m (750ft) of ascent – if you're going well, go for it. The two routes converge again at the Sulzenauhütte. This is an audaciously positioned building, perched on the rim of a huge corrie and a good point at which to rest a while and recover from the last part of the walk. It is possible to descend from here if the weather or some other factor makes it necessary, via Sulzegg, the route being described in Walk 18.

From the Sulzenauhütte there is some more climbing for a while at least. The walk follows a well-marked path which gradually climbs into a small valley, which in turn leads up to a small lake, the Grünausee (Green Lake). The person who named this little gem was either colour blind, or in fact witnessed lighting or other physical conditions which caused it to look green,

The superb view of the glacier from Beiljoch, en route to the Nürnburger Hütte

as nowadays it seems to look distinctly blue – rather a strong blue in fact. Whatever colour you judge it to be, it will undoubtedly look very beautiful, set against a background of scree, rock and high, dazzlingly white glaciers.

Right at the apex of the lake, the route takes a sharp left-hand turn and leads up to a path junction, near a cluster of small lakes. The Nürnburger Hütte can be reached via either route, but the right-hand one is by far the easiest, crossing the ridge ahead via the Niederl col and leaving only a short but steep descent to the hut. The left-hand branch goes via a route which is over 120m (400ft) higher, but gives access to the Maierspitze, which can easily be bagged in 15 minutes from the ridge high point. It is the descent down on to the Nürnburger side which is tricky, but fixed cables ease the way. This way should really only be done by those with a little experience of this sort of easy climbing.

Assuming the normal, right-hand route has been chosen, you will be able to make out the large crucifix from quite a distance, but reaching it is another matter. It is further than it seems and the last section up to the ridge is steep, though fortunately short and containing some fixed cables. The descent too is deceptively long and some loose sections ensure that concentration cannot lapse until the hut, which is in the middle of a kaleidoscopic stonescape, is reached.

The hut itself is modern and particularly stoutly built, blending in very well with its stern and bleak surroundings. Above it stands a huge rock wall, and well above, the huge Wilder Freiger Glacier – part of the biggest glacier system in the Stubai, with the peak of the same name topping this. The Nürnburger Hütte is a good start point for an ascent of this 3,419m (11,217ft) mountain, and it is reputed to have the finest view in the whole area. It is climbed at all times of the year, but especially in spring by ski-touring parties when the glacier is easier to cross than in the summer, because many more crevasses are exposed and route-finding can become a problem.

The descent from the hut presents no particular problems other than making heavy packs seem heavier and tired knees stiffer, and you'll probably be grateful for the well-made path, and the many hours of effort which must have gone into building it. The valley is about 1 1/2 hours away and the section can be split at Bsuchalm, where refreshments are available. One feature of many other huts can be seen here – the capacity to send rucksacks up and down by cableway. Indeed, many people take advantage of this service. From Bsuchalm, a steady descent on a wide track continues the downward journey, which can be speeded up for its final section by taking a smaller path off to the left after about 15 minutes. This avoids the final long zigzags of the road and brings you out near the parking area and bus stop at the bottom of the main track.

Walk 20 Dresdner Hütte via Wilde Grube

Map no:	Kompass 1:25,000; Stubaital
Walking time:	4 hours
Grading:	M
Highest altitude:	2,506m (8,222ft)
Lowest altitude:	1,721m (5,646ft)

This is a high-level walk which could have extensive areas of snow early in the season, and indeed could be prone to snow in its upper sections at any time of year. It is therefore recommended that ice axes be carried when there is likely to be snow on the route. In snow-free conditions there are no problems as the way is clear and well marked.

The Walk

This fine walk starts amongst the crowds of colourfully-clad skiers, clomping their way up the road to the start of the gondola system which gives access to the glaciers. This point, known as Mutterbergalm (the highest point in the valley to which it is possible to drive), can be reached by car or by the Stubai bus. Across to the right is an impressive rocky gorge which normally contains a torrent of white water, but most walkers will not linger here, preferring instead to get away from this busy area. Walk up past the gondola station and follow a track which leads off towards the steep hillside under the cableway. After crossing a bridge on the right, take the track which leads back to the right and follow it steeply for about 20 minutes to a flatter area which is reminiscent of British walking – it's wet! By now, excellent views are opening up both ahead and back down the valley, and the bustle of the Mutterbergalm is becoming a memory.

We now find ourselves in a beautiful upper valley, covered in bilberry and stunted pine with a scattering of taller trees. A number of long, white waterfalls tumble down into this basin and the usual quota of cud-chewing cows laze about in the drier areas. The best route here is to keep to the left of the stream until a recent (1989) ski track is reached. This new ski

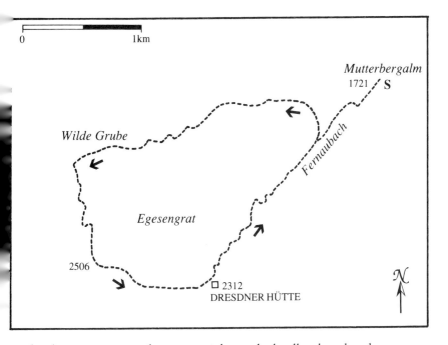

development is very unfortunate as it has undoubtedly taken the edge away from a most beautiful valley. The track is gentle at first, but then steepens for a short way before levelling out into another high valley. Pause for a rest! Again, numerous streams and waterfalls rumble down into the grey river and again, the new ski road forges up the valley – maybe it will look better after it has had time to settle in. Just where the track steepens again (good picnic places by the river), a well-marked, narrow path leads off to the left and ascends the steep hillside in a series of short zigzags which mean the ascent is never as horrendous as it first appears. The views now are excellent – back to Habicht and across to the Mutterberger Seespitze and the Hölltalspitze in particular.

This narrow path eventually levels out into yet another tiny valley, surrounded by cliffs and with an impressive torrent running down its right-hand side. Continue along this waymarked route, periodically joining the new ski road until a short rocky step (well marked) leads up into a final small, flat-bottomed valley. This is a great place. The panorama is excellent, the feel is that of the high mountains and the route continues to surprise and impress. Follow the short but flat floor of this valley and then ascend a series of zigzags which climb an unlikely looking rock and scree slope. Then ascend a short rocky section which contains some totally unnecessary wire safety rope to

On the path up through the Wilde Grube

arrive at a superb col, where the views really open up. The top of a huge boulder on the right gives an excellent rest and picnic site. On a good day, this is a place to linger, where high mountain tops can be picked out and named and where the atmosphere of these high mountain passes can be savoured to the full.

The descent to the Dresdner Hütte is straightforward and should take 15 – 20 minutes. This hut is a busy place, being served by the gondola which caters for tourists, walkers and skiers alike. Despite this, it is a pleasant place to sit for lunch and the side of the hut which faces up towards the glaciers is a sun trap *par excellence*. The food and beer is similar in price to most other places and the hut has a self-service cafeteria inside. Early in the season, there is likely to be plenty of snow in the huge bowl above the hut, but later in the year, this disappears to leave a huge, scree-filled slope which resembles an enormous quarrying or mining area. Apparently, this hillside was devastated recently by some massive floods and landslides, which explains the man-made appearance. It can hardly be described as beautiful, but it exudes an image of scale and rawness which is in some ways equally enlightening.

There is a choice of route from here on. Either follow Walk 18, which involves a further arduous ascent and a very long descent in wild terrain – perhaps more suited to those who are more experienced and who had an early start – or follow the path from the rear of the Dresdner Hütte which zigzags easily down to the left of the gondola (looking down), in about 50 minutes back to the Mutterbergalm. Of course, there is the other option of taking the gondola back down, and there is no disgrace in this, although the feeling of a day out is more complete if the descent is made on foot.

In snow-free conditions and in good weather, this is a fine route which any reasonably fit walker can enjoy. It provides good exercise and some superb views as well as some stark contrasts in terms of man-made development in these high Alpine regions and we would do well to consider the further implications of this in relation to both these and our own mountains.

Walk 21   Dresdner Hütte – Daunkogel Ostlicher

Map no:	Kompass 1:25,000; Stubaital
Walking time:	6 hours
Grading:	C
Highest altitude:	3,332m (10,932ft)
Lowest altitude:	1,721m (5,646ft) (or 2,302m/7,552ft if chair used to Dresdner)

This is the hardest route in the book and involves reaching a fairly high summit by means of a glacier crossing and the ascent of a short ridge. Would be ascensionists should have experience of glacier travel and basic rope work as the ridge, though never difficult, is exposed. In full snow cover it is best left to experienced climbers or those with a local guide.

The Walk

At the very head of the Stubaital, the land steepens into a vast headwall of rock, scree and ice which leads out on to the high glaciers where year-round skiing takes place. Above these glaciers a number of peaks stand proud, lying right on the watershed between the Stubaital and the Otztal. The most notable summits are the shovel-shaped Schaufelspitze, the Stubaier Wildspitze and the Ostlicher and Westlicher Daunkogel. The ascent of the Ostlicher Daunkogel makes a fine introduction to climbing the area's more serious mountains and it gives a fine route amidst strong glacial scenery with magnificent summit views.

It must be stressed that the route always presents more problems than any other in this guide, and it should ONLY BE ATTEMPTED BY EXPERIENCED PARTIES OR WITH A LOCAL GUIDE.

The start point is the Dresdner Hütte, which can be reached by a variety of routes from Mutterbergalm (see Walk 20). The best idea is to aim to reach the hut in late afternoon, permitting a leisurely evening before the next day's ascent. Use this time to check out the start of the walk, to eliminate any mistakes taking place in the poor light of your dawn start.

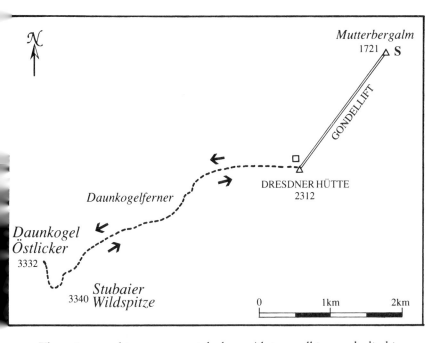

There is something very special about Alpine walking and climbing which goes beyond the mere ascent of the chosen mountain. Everything, from the snoring in the hut, the anxious half-sleep and the excited anticipation of the day to come, to the chill of the early morning Alpine air and the sharp crunch of crampons on the frozen snow, gives a lasting memory which even long absences can never diminish. Walking out into the early morning twilight, from which a rosy dawn slowly emerges, followed in turn by a fresh new mountain day, is a quite unforgettable experience.

Most Alpine walks involve an early start to take advantage of the lower temperatures which mean harder snow, easier progress and more safety. The aim is to get back down to the hut for lunch time, avoiding the main heat of the day and giving a short rest period before the descent back down to the valley.

This walk will take an average of $3 - 3^1/_2$ hours from the hut, and as the first sections are quite easy, a start an hour or so before dawn is recommended. To leave much earlier is unnecessary for a route of this nature, and an experienced party could easily leave much later. However, to experience the full delight of this type of route, a pre-dawn start is a good idea, following the route you checked out the previous night.

From the hut, a good path leads westwards, crossing a stream just after a junction (the right fork here leads to the Wilde Grube, a possible descent). The path leads up on to the Daunkogel glacier (Daunkopfferner) which is ascended in a west-south-west direction, passing ski tows, the only drawback to the walk – but if you're out early enough they won't be running. Remember that crossing this or any glacier involves route-finding difficulties where crevasses have to be avoided. Experience in basic rope work and the ability to perform crevasse rescue is essential, as are crampons and ice axe. On the glacier is a rocky island, at 2,993m (9,819ft) which our route bypasses ideally on the right. The summits ahead are becoming obvious now and we aim for the col between the Stubaier Wildspitze and the Ostlicher Daunkogel. This col marks the end of the easy section and the start of the more difficult ridge. Its true difficulty, as in the crossing of the glacier, depends upon how much snow is around. In climbing terms, the ridge is graded F (Facile), the easiest Alpine grade. It starts easily enough, and in reality has only one tricky section, a short rock step which is turned on the right. The route is always well-defined and easy to follow, though the sense of exposure (feeling of height) is considerable. The summit arrives fairly quickly – about $^1/_2$ hour from the base of the ridge, and you are greeted by the usual huge crucifix, so familiar in these parts. The views really are magnificent in all directions and on a sunny morning there is a lot to try to identify – good practice in the use of map and compass. If this is your first Alpine summit – climb as opposed to walk, you won't need me to tell you how you feel and if you are an experienced Alpiniste, the good views and ambience of the situation will make up for the lack of serious difficulties.

Take your time up there, make the most it, eat and drink and forget the hard slog up the glacier and the early morning yawns! Eventually though it will be time to consider the descent. To leave the summit, it is necessary to descend the same ridge as you came up as the other routes are considerably harder. Descending rock is always trickier than ascending the same piece, so take care and make sure your concentration levels are as high as they were for the ascent. The glacier route can be reversed, or alternatively, it is possible to walk from the col at the foot of the ridge in an easterly direction under the north-east face of the Stubaier Wildspitze (beware of avalanche danger), crossing ski tows and lifts with care, to reach the Eisgrat Restaurant. There is an easy path down the west side of the ridge beneath this place which leads in one hour back to the Dresdner Hütte. There are three options for the final descent from here. The easiest option is to hop on to the cable-car. This may well feel like a good idea at the time, but if you have some energy left, a walk down is possible, either by following the path which runs under and just to one side of the cable-car (50 minutes), or via the Wilde Grube route. This is the most agreeable descent, but the fact that you first have to retrace your steps uphill for 15 minutes before starting the path down will probably lead to dissent and potential mutiny from some members of the party. If you do manage to summon up the energies and interest, just reverse the route description for the ascent by this way under Walk 20.

Whichever route you take, given good weather, this should have been an enjoyable day which may have planted the seeds of further exploration. Alpine mountaineering is a fine business indeed, but do remember that it is also a serious business, one which demands fitness, planning, and a variety of skills. My advice is to go about it in the right way by taking advantage of recognised courses such as those run by the British Mountaineering Council, or the services of a qualified and professional Mountain Guide. Persuading an experienced friend to take you under his or her wing is another popular way of starting off on an Alpine career. Maybe you'll be able to look back on this little peak in years to come as the one which set you on the road to greater things, or perhaps as the culmination of your experiences in the mountains. Whichever, I don't think you'll be disappointed.

Walk 22   Mutterbergalm – Grabaalm – Ranalt

Map no:	Kompass 1:25,000; Stubaital
Walking time:	2 hours 30 minutes
Grading:	E
Highest altitude:	1,721m (5,646ft) (the route goes downhill)
Lowest altitude:	1,303m (4,275ft)

A walk which is especially suitable for an off day or evening, being thoroughly downhill and for the most part on easy ground. It is particularly exciting when the river is in spate, but don't get too close!

The Walk

Although the road up the Stubai valley is a close companion for the duration of this walk, the path is normally just far enough away from it, and the river noisy enough to reduce its potential impact, enabling the walk to be enjoyed without distraction. The best way to undertake it is to use the Stubai bus for the journey to Mutterbergalm, walk down the valley as far as time and energy permits and then use the Stubai bus again for the journey back to your lodgings. For runners, the full length of the valley makes a pleasant day out, as much of the run is downhill or on the flat, and one of the most important factors in choosing this route is that the user can choose from numerous 'opt out' points along the way.

Start from the bottom of the car parks at Mutterbergalm and follow the narrow path which leads down towards the right-hand side of the river (looking downstream). Almost immediately, the road which is running parallel, is hidden by an avalanche tunnel – fair warning of the potential problems faced here in winter. There is a huge cone of debris, above the tunnel, more testimony to the avalanche problem. Many years of local knowledge and experience has now minimized the risks of damage and obstruction, but despite fairly accurate prediction, avalanches can still strike in places where they have never been known before, and their destructive powers have to be seen to be believed. On the slope above this avalanche

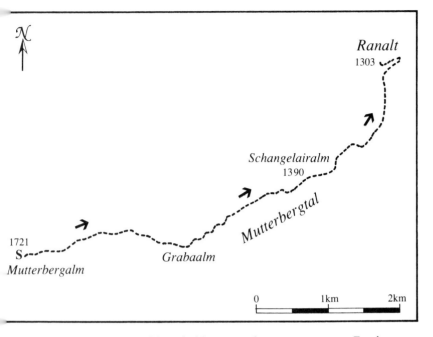

tunnel, the dangers would probably come from two sources. Firstly, a northerly wind would deposit large quantities of snow on to the face above the tunnel, and with a steep angle such as this, slides will be frequent, depending on the nature of the underlying surface. If the snow depth is great, this type of new snow avalanche could be very powerful. The other problem here could well be that because the hillside faces south, thaw conditions may create wet snow avalanches, where huge slips occur due to a layer of water or thawing snow creating a sliding surface on which the avalanche could move. These comments are a gross simplification of the theory and practice of avalanche prediction, but they will give the reader a basic idea of what could happen here. Anyone interested further would find *The Avalanche Enigma* by Colin Fraser to be valuable and fascinating reading – and guaranteed to ensure you never take chances with the 'white death'.

Back on to the path now, and yet more natural devastation to be witnessed, this time as a result of the vast quantities of water which can flow down this river. When heavy rain combines with melting snow, the huge catchment area of the river can give rise to volumes of water which create immense floods, and damage to the landscape on a massive scale, an example of which can now be seen right in front of you, and in fact continues for much of this upper section of the river. Its banks are gouged and torn, huge boulders lie

The view down the river from a spot near Mutterbergalm

strewn across a wide area, whilst once grassy pastures are covered with mud and scree. Not pretty perhaps, but unavoidably engaging.

Our path continues down a steeper section, narrow and very different from the wide forest trails that make up so many of the walks in the lower regions of the valley. This soon gives way to coniferous forest, whose floor is carpeted with cushions of bilberry and fern and in which the tree cover exhibits a wide range of age and size, unusual in an area where forestry normally commands an even age grouping. In this section, the path to Sulzegg is passed and shortly afterwards, the booming of the big waterfall can be heard before it can be seen. Between the waterfall and the road is Grabaalm, the first refreshment stop (if one is required), and the path leads to near the foot of these great falls. Always impressive, they are especially noisy and swollen after rain, but they may also turn a dirty grey/brown.

Beyond here, our route keeps to the same side of the river and contours beneath some large, wet, vegetated and uninviting cliffs, the lower spurs of the Maierspitze, before rising and remaining quite high, steering well clear of the devastated river bed below. Further along, the road is met and crossed, the path keeping on the right of the river between it and the road, before it rejoins the road at the point where the main path to the Nürnburger Hütte leaves it. This is always a busy area with lots of parked cars, and the Stubai bus stops here. A short distance further, a road leads off to the right, follow this and turn immediately left on to a path which contours down to Ranalt, which at 1,303m (4,275ft) is 420m (1,378ft) lower than the start point. From here, there are a number of options. Back on the main road is the Stubai bus stop, but if time and circumstances permit, the walk can easily be continued along to Volderau. The route to here follows the road for a short way until just before the avalanche tunnel, when a path leads off to the left, ascending and then descending beyond the tunnel to Falbeson. Crossing the road here leads to a gentle forest track which meanders down to Volderau, emerging opposite the campsite entrance. Again, the Stubai bus stops here and options are still available for a continuation down the valley, though most people will have had enough by now, and may be settling for a well-earned drink in the locals bar here.

No one would pretend that this has been a high-level mountain walk, but it is nonetheless entertaining and varied, well worth the effort and particularly valuable for an 'off day' or for poor weather.

Walk 23 Mutterbergalm – Dresdner Hütte – Eisgrat – Glacier – Return

Map no:	Kompass 1:25,000; Stubaital
Walking time:	4 hours
Grading:	M
Highest altitude:	3,160m (10,367ft)
Lowest altitude:	2,850m (9,350ft) (height of top lift)

Using the chair-lift system at Mutterbergalm which serves tourists and mountaineers as well as skiers, enables ordinary walkers to experience the breathtaking views and icy atmosphere of glacier travel. In addition to this, there is a well-marked and safe path from the Eisgrat to the Jochdohle – 'the highest snack bar in Austria'. It must be remembered that it can be considerably colder at this altitude than in the valley, so adequate clothing must be taken, and walkers should also have good sunglasses as the glare can be anything from uncomfortable to painful and dangerous. Reasonable boots and gaiters are also pretty much essential as the summer sun quickly softens the surface. Ski sticks are useful to walk with. Early or late in the season, or in exceptional weather in summer, the walk may be inadvisable due to ice, deep snow or extremes of wind or temperature. If in doubt, ask at the ticket office, where advice is freely available.

The Walk

The day starts off from Mutterbergalm, which is reached by car or by the Stubai bus. At the very end of the valley, this is the start point for the glacier skiers and for walkers and mountaineers visiting the Dresdner Hütte and a variety of high peaks. On this particular walk, I recommend that the chair-lift be used for the ascent on to the glacier and also in descent for those who do not relish the thought of the walk down which, though easy, is long and knee-jarring, because the terrain is exclusively rocky. (Just in case you prefer a warm up to the day by walking to the Dresdner Hütte, *consult* Walk 20 for an alternative description.)

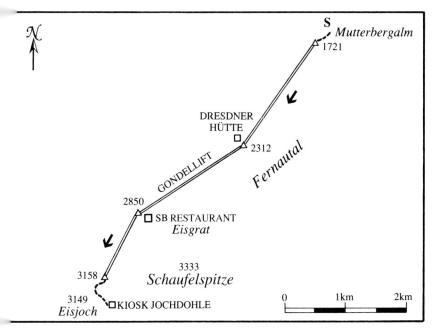

N

S
Mutterbergalm
1721

DRESDNER
HÜTTE
□ 2312

GONDELLIFT

Fernautal

2850
□ SB RESTAURANT
Eisgrat

3333
3158
Schaufelspitze

3149
□KIOSK JOCHDOHLE
Eisjoch

0   1km   2km

Assuming you have resisted the temptation to consult Walk 20, climb aboard the cable-car and enjoy a swift ascent from 1,720m (5,640ft) to 2,300m (7,500ft) – Dresdner Hütte – and then on to the Eisgrat, at 2,850m (9,350ft). Enjoy the ride up, the views are ever changing and ever wider. **Note:** When you get off the lift, make sure you have all your belongings – it's easy to leave gloves or glasses on the seat in the rush to get out of the car.

The Eisgrat is an amalgamation of shops, ski school and restaurant, perched between the Schaufel and Daunkogel Glaciers and commanding an exceptional panorama. The building itself is modern but not unattractive, probably providing one of the better examples of high mountain architecture, although a building of this size is always going to be intrusive in such a location. Out in front, a variety of tows pull skiers high on to the glacier, giving access to excellent skiing throughout the year. You may also see Snowboarders riding a single wide ski and standing sideways, like a skateboarder. This latest type of ski is very popular with young skiers and the Stubai glacier ski schools hold special week-long courses to learn how to enjoy this new sensation. Dominating the skyline is the Schaufelspitze, just left of the main ski tows and across to the right the Stubaier Wildspitze, the Östlicher Daunkogel and the Westlichen Daunkogel form an impressive barrier.

The walk to the Jochdole is gentle and well marked and you will normally be following a heavily trodden path, although the fact that you are over 3,333m (10,900ft) could lead to mild altitude problems such as headaches and being slightly out of breath. The route generally follows a line just to the left of the left-hand skiing piste, by a prominent fence and leads up to the col at which the tows finish. The hut is now just down the other side of this pass to the left. On a good day, the views are exceptional, incorporating parts of the Dolomites and the Otztal Alps, and you will no doubt want to extend your stay at this high level sun trap but watch out for glare and sunburn. It is about 55 minutes from the Eisgrat.

When you retrace your steps back down to the Eisgrat, it is worth having a good look at these glaciated areas, whose appearance will change considerably, depending on the time of year and the weather. In the summer of 1989, the high temperatures and lack of snowfall turned the glaciers grey and revealed hundreds of crevasses. These splits in the ice, which can vary from a few inches wide to huge caverns, hundreds of feet deep are the real enemy of the high-level mountaineer. In certain conditions, they remain totally or partially covered, making it difficult to anticipate their whereabouts and creating serious problems for skiers and climbers. Crevasses occur mainly in the parts of the glacier where the surface flows over a convex slope, the ice naturally splitting as it does so, whilst concave slopes are often much safer as the ice is being compressed. Having said this, there is no really safe place on a glacier unless a route has been well chosen and is constantly monitored (such as the route you are on). Avalanches will also sweep down from certain slopes, such as the steep north face of the Schaufelspitze, as masses of unstable snow part company with the subsurface in a wide range of conditions. You may well see avalanche debris at the foot of this or some of the other north-facing slopes hereabouts. High-level areas such as this are also prone to very quick weather changes – high winds or violent storms can spring from nowhere, a lowering cloud base can severely reduce visibility and snowfall can create whiteout conditions in which all sense of direction and angle of slope is lost. Having said all this, a good day with a settled weather forecast will enable you to enjoy your day out in comparative safety.

Having returned to the Eisgrat, you may catch the cable-car back down, or try the descent on foot, which follows conspicuous red spots of paint, at first behind the station, then progressively further left (looking downhill), sweeping in a curve to reach the Dresdner Hütte in about an hour. Again, there is a well-marked path down from here, although the cable-car is still there as an easy option.

Walk 24   Gschnitz – Innsbrucker Hütte – Habicht – Gschnitz

Map no:	Kompass 1:25,000; Stubaital
Walking time:	3 to 6 hours (depending on the route and whether you use the chair-lift both ways)
Grading:	C
Highest altitude:	3,277m (10,757ft)
Lowest altitude:	1,242m (4,075ft)

In this walk, there is a height difference of 1,130m (3,700ft) between Gschnitz and the hut, and 900m (2,950ft) of ascent from the hut to the summit of Habicht.

It is marked as a difficult C, indicating that easy climbing is involved. However, the ascent of Habicht is one of the hardest routes in the scope of this book and it should not be undertaken without scrambling and glacier crossing experience. Therefore, the walk can be varied by missing out the route on to Habicht and descending into the Pinnis valley, in which case it falls within the moderate category.

The Walk

Habicht is one of the best known peaks in the Stubai, and it was the second major peak to be ascended in the area after the Strahlkogel, in 1836. At 3,277m (10,751ft), it is one of the highest peaks, though by no means the highest in the Tyrol, as was once thought. If you intend to climb it, you should have experience of scrambling and easy climbing and you should be conversant with the techniques involved in glacier travel. Needless to say, on a mountain of this size the weather will always be prone to sudden changes, and extensive snow cover may occur even in the summer months. As a peak, it has much to recommend it. A variety of routes (of which this is the easiest), a small glacier and superb views which give the feel of being on a bigger and more difficult peak. If you're not sure of your ability, why not enjoy the day with a local guide. Many guides speak perfect English, are highly skilled and know

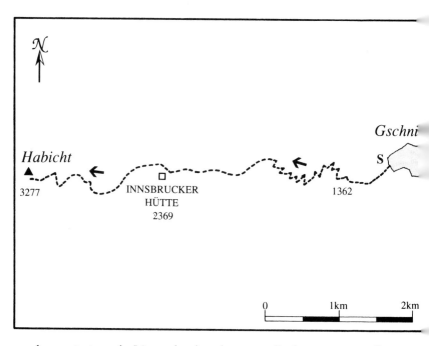

the area intimately. It's worth a thought, especially if you are in a small group, when the cost may not be as high.

The village of Gschnitz, can be reached by car via Steinach. A bus service from Innsbruck is also available. If you intend to descend into the Pinnis valley instead of retracing your steps down to Gschnitz, it is important to ensure that adequate transport arrangements are made, as Neustift and Gschnitz are a long way apart by road!

To start the walk, locate the *Berghof* in Gschnitz. Behind here, a well marked path leaves the road at a crossroad-like junction and soon climbs steeply through pleasant meadows. If you are only walking as far as the hut today – which most people will – take your time and prolong the ascent, there is plenty of botanical interest here, and you will pass numerous hay barns, whose presence seems to encourage relaxation. Despite the numerous zigzags, the path still feels steep and it is with some relief that there is a slight levelling out as you reach the southern edge of the limestone crags and screes of the Kalkwand. The route levels off even more, and continues to traverse along rocky terrain to the Pinnisjoch, where the Innsbrucker Hütte is situated. After an ascent of 1,130m (3,700ft) a good rest is called for, after which you can think about looking briefly at the route you will follow the next morning up on to Habicht.

*The upper Pinnis valley with the Innsbrucker Hütte
located in the col in the centre of the picture*

The hut is very pleasant, relatively inexpensive considering its situation and possesses a congenial ambience. It stands proudly in a high level col between two fine valleys and is really worth a visit in its own right. In 1989, it was under £10 for a good meal with wine, breakfast and overnight accommodation.

The route of ascent described – the East Side Ordinary Route – is the easiest on the mountain, being given a grade of F, or Facile, the easiest of the Alpine grades. In reality it is little more than a well-marked steep path, with some scrambling and sections of fixed gear (mostly the usual steel cables), and a short glacier crossing.

From the hut, follow the path in a westerly direction to the foot of the broad south-east ridge. The route winds steeply on, mostly on easy, slabby rocks with fixed cables wherever there is any difficulty, until after a section overlooking the Pinnistal side or the mountain, you move up to the edge of the *petite* Habicht glacier. There is normally a well-worn path leading westwards across it to a final section of rocky ground which leads without further difficulty to the summit. Though never hard, the way up has been varied and interesting, presenting different aspects and views of the surrounding peaks and culminating in an airy summit from which you can identify dozens of neighbouring peaks.

For the descent, reverse the way you have just followed, taking care to avoid any deviation to the north east on the glacier as it ends rather suddenly! Though a fast party can do the ascent in a couple of hours, $2^1/_2$ hours represents a good time and 3 hours is quite acceptable.

There are three good alternatives from here. The first is to descend back down to Gschnitz and enjoy the comforts of the valley, which has its merits. The second is to walk down to Neustift via the Pinnis valley, having previously arranged the right combination of transport and accommodation. Though rather long, this is a lovely descent which is steep only at its start. The main valley is a real joy to descend, especially in its upper part where the Pinnisalm provides refreshment in a superb high pasture setting. Lower down there is a huge boulder on the path side on which to test your climbing skills, then a long descent on a good track leads back down to the valley – about 3 hours in total, at an average pace allowing time for eating, drinking and sunbathing.

The third option is to climb the Ilmspitze, an impressive little peak on the opposite side of the hut to Habicht. This involves an easy '*via ferrata* ' – a Dolomitic name which is entirely appropriate here, as the rock architecture is so reminiscent of the bigger Italian mountains to the south east. These 'iron ways' as the translation hints, are routes on which iron ladders, hand and foot holds and steel cables are fixed to make the going easier. Initially, it takes some getting used to, however, once you're into the swing of things, you tend to accept that it is a part of continental mountaineering, and some of the routes ascended in this way are highly enjoyable. The way up the Ilmspitze is indeed very enjoyable, though not hard and the overall character of the climb is extremely appealing. This route could be done in the same day as Habicht by a fit party, but many would prefer to relax and spend another night in the hut, before making the summit the following day and then continuing to descend back to the valley. After all, if you've made the effort to walk all the way up to the hut, why not grab an extra walk while you're there?

Walk 25 Schönberg – Gleinser Hof – Alpengasthaus Maria Waldras – Mieders – Fulpmes – Neustift – Telfes – Kreith – Mieders – Schönberg

Map no:	Kompass 1:25,000; Stubaital
Walking time:	—
Grading:	M
Highest altitude:	1,650m (5,413ft)
Lowest altitude:	1,026m (3,366ft)

This walk is best accomplished as a ride! It is a relatively easy ride, though the first part of the day consists of a fairly steady ascent which non-cyclists will find quite a challenge.

The Ride

Schönberg is the starting point, and is situated right at the foot of the Stubai valley, although the route is circular and can be started at any point, depending on whether you are hiring bikes and where from. The advantage of doing it the way described here is that the main ascent is tackled early in the day.

The village is in a fine position, elevated on a hillside (the name itself means Lovely Hill) with excellent views of the Stubai and Tuxer peaks. Because it is right at the start of the Stubai valley it is somewhat neglected by most walkers, who prefer to press on higher into the mountains. It is the start point for a route which is described as one to ride round rather than walk, though walking it is equally possible, if rather long. The terrain and paths of the lower part of the Stubai are superb for mountain biking. The ascents are never too steep while the descents can be fast and exhilarating. Surfaces are generally solid and stony rather than soft and muddy, giving rise to few erosion problems and a general feeling that mountain bikes are not looked upon as nuisances, especially as there is plenty of room for walkers, bikers and everyone else with very little conflict. It would be good to keep the situation

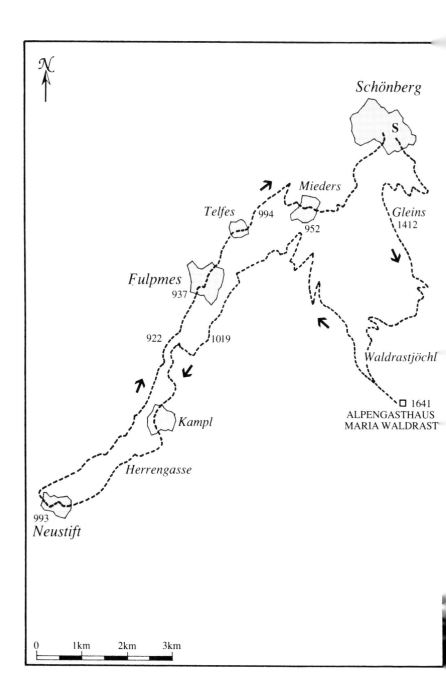

this way, so please keep only to the good, hard tracks and respect wildlife and other path users.

Bikes can be hired from a number of locations such as Neustift and Fulpmes and are relatively inexpensive. If you've never been on a mountain type bike before, be prepared for a few differences from the normal racer. Firstly, the rider adopts a more upright position for increased stability. Then, the wide tyres and less streamlined shapes make the bike harder to ride at speed on the road. However, it's off-road where the bikes come into their own. Eighteen or twenty-one gears will make pedalling up most gradients easy work, though progress may seem slow, and the wide tyres make light of rough ground. Despite all the gears, they are easy to ride and the brakes fitted are normally very effective.

In the middle of Schönberg, a minor road crosses the main one just before a bend to the right (when travelling north-east). Turn right here and follow this road under the motorway. After a short way in an open area, we enter the forest and take a right fork on the *Rodelbahn* which then zigzags up to the Gleinser Hof. This is an unrelenting ascent and those low gears will be getting plenty of use! Once in the vicinity of the Gleinser Hof, the gradients ease for a while and you contour along a good track, occasionally ascending slightly, to join another track which comes in from the right. Keeping left and following signs for the Ochsenhütte the path zigzags, rises, traverses and descends until a junction is reached. Fork left here, away from the Oschenhütte and towards Alpengasthaus Maria Waldras. Though this involves a slight descent, it is worth it. There is a monastery next door which attracted 40,000 pilgrims annually in the eighteenth century, and the inn is a good start point for an ascent of Serles. After your well-earned break, turn round and retrace your steps (or wheel tracks), to follow a long descent on good roads through the forest, right down to the chair-lift station at Mieders. The loss of height involved totals 750m (2,460ft), so be prepared for a fast and exhilarating ride! (In actual fact the descent road is a long one and the gradient is never too steep, so a moderate speed can easily be maintained if required.)

There are a variety of routes from here up to Neustift, the highest point in the valley to which we ride. The best is probably to turn left at the chair-lift station and go down to the Café Jagerhausl, which is just before the main road. A left turn here leads along the Ebnersteig and into Medrazer Stille. Wend down on to the main road here, cross it, then turn left along the old road which rejoins the main road after a short way. A short section along the main road leads to Kampl. Turn left here and work away up through the village before contouring above the road and descending into Neustift. Time for lunch.

From here, it is possible to keep on the opposite side of the valley to that which most of the route has been on so far. A road leads out of Neustift past Schöne Aussicht and down to Rain. A short excursion on to the main road and you can turn off to the left again along a minor road which leads through the hay meadows to Medraz. A short ride then leads in turn to Fulpmes, and then to Telfes, where I suggest a stop for afternoon tea and cakes. The route from Telfes then wanders down to Mieders, from where a short ascent and a contouring track lead back to Schönberg.

There are obviously many variations possible on this route. More hardy riders can consider the ascent of the track to the Elferhütte, and a thrilling descent down the sledging track into the Pinnis valley. Whatever your wish, there is always a route to suit and plenty of cut off points if time runs out or an afternoon thunderstorm spreads its dark shadow. Please remember to show respect for other path users if you are on a mountain bike, and keep to the well surfaced routes to avoid erosion and wildlife disturbance. Above all, have a good day!

Walks 26–32   The Stubai Horseshoe

Map no: Kompass 1:25,000; Stubaital

Walking time: 1 day per walk

Grading: D

Highest altitude: 2,754m (9,035ft)

Lowest altitude: The start of the walk is at 1,051m (3,448ft)
NOTE: As this is a multi-day route, it has many more variations in
            height within the figures given above.

It will take 7 days for the full tour around the rim of the Stubai valley from
Fulpmes to the Dresdner Hütte and back via the Innsbrucker Hütte, though
it could be done quicker (or slower) if desired. There is a base route
throughout, which can be varied from time to time to take in the occasional
summit or to enable the overall route to be lengthened or shortened at will.

This walk has an easy D for the easiest route, but is a little more difficult
at times if variations are taken. Nowhere is it particularly tricky, though there
is some hard walking and some easy scrambling.

The Walk

This walk is rather like an overgrown version of the Langdale, Snowdon or
Fairfield horseshoes in the UK, and it has attraction in its line, its variety and
its views. The sections between huts can be done as individual day walks and
the entire route is always relatively safe and escapable.

One of the great advantages of longer distance hut to hut walks is that it
is not necessary to carry all the normal paraphernalia required for multi-day
walks. Cooking equipment, tents, sleeping bags and boxfuls of food can be
happily jettisoned into the pile marked 'unnecessary', at least for the
moment. Instead, you can walk with a minimum of gear, travelling light and
fast, unencumbered by excessive weight and bulk. This is surely the best way
to travel in the hills and those of you who would normally carry your own gear
will almost without exception appreciate the freedom which this form of
route provides. Its only drawback is that you have to pay for the privilege!

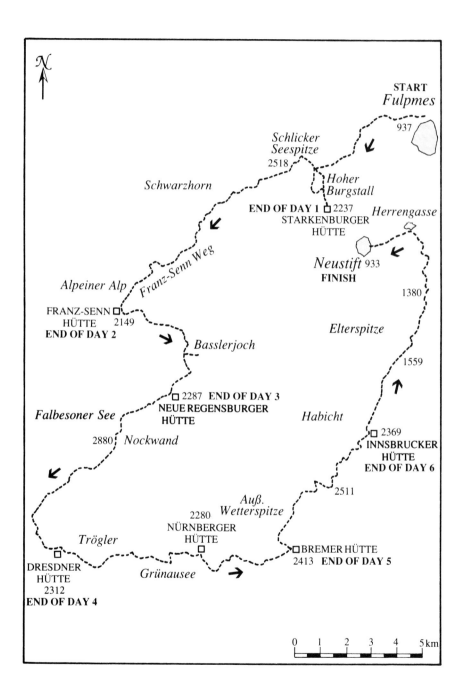

Fortunately the accommodation and food is really quite reasonably priced considering the logistics involved in building and stocking these high level hostels. All the huts used on this walk are of a high standard and they will certainly surprise those who are used to staying in some of the smaller French huts. As a guide, it was around £10 for bed, breakfast and a hearty evening meal with wine in 1989. I would recommend that the hut to hut tour be undertaken outside the main holiday periods if at all possible, to avoid the problems associated with overcrowding both in the huts and on the paths.

It is possible to do the horseshoe either way round, though I will describe it in an anti-clockwise manner, starting at Fulpmes. The walk is described without the use of lifts, though it can be shortened in places if they are used. The first objective is the Starkenburger Hütte, which sits high above Neustift, below the Hoher Burgstall. To get there, you begin by walking up to the Schlicker Alm, starting from the chair-lift station in Fulpmes and then attaining the hut via first a forest road, and then a gentler track up through open pastures and sparse woodland. (This, and the following section on to the Hoher Burgstall is a reversal of the return part of Walk 9.) From the Schlicker Alm, continue up to the Zirmachalm, from where a path leads off to the right, ascending a long though not too steep valley. This leads right up to a col known as Schlicker Scharte. A long traverse then leads leftwards, under the crags and across the screes, eventually coming directly beneath the Hoher Burgstall. Although the front of this peak presents a formidable looking blocky buttress, the ascent of it is very straightforward, and scree and easy scrambling to the right of the main crag leads up to the summit ridge and then to the large crucifix on the summit. In descent, reverse the route a short way, then turn left and descend passing lots of avalanche barriers to join a good path which leads leftwards to the Starkenburger Hütte. Night one can be spent here. Allow $5^{1}/_{2}$ – 6 hours for getting to the hut.

The next day's walk will take you all the way along to the Franz Senn Hütte. The bulk of the way consists of a gently undulating traverse, part of the Franz Senn Weg, beneath the Schwarzhorn and the Schaldersspitze. From the hut, backtrack along the path towards the Hoher Burgstall (path 116) and keep to the left, avoiding the path which you should have descended yesterday. The path works round a ridge and then climbs to the Schlicker Scharte, before rising gently to Seejochl, which is nicely positioned above the little Oberberger lakes. A number of paths meet at this point, the one you want bears to the left, and rises to a maximum height of 2,589m (8,494ft) (this is path 117). The next good stopping point is Seduckalm, a small hut which provides the only refreshment point along the way. This place is reached via a long and gently varied traverse which loses 340m

On day 2 of the Horseshoe

The approach to the Franz Senn Hütte

The tiny church just above the Schlicker Alm

(1,100ft) along its length. The views across to the east and north are excellent and a good variety of flowers can be seen. From Seduckalm, continue traversing (reversal of part of Walk 14), passing streams and a wide amphitheatre before finally joining up with path 132 and descending to the Franz Senn Hütte. Hut to hut, the journey is $4^1/_2 - 5^1/_2$ leisurely hours, with the promise of a relaxing evening ahead and an exciting day tomorrow.

Day three is a short one. The objective is the Neue Regensburger Hütte which lies the far side of the Schrimmennieder col. The huge sweeps of scree and broken rock which hide the path leading up to this point can be seen well by walking a short way to the north-east from the Franz Senn Hütte towards the Horntaler Joch. In fact, it is worth a ten minute evening stroll to examine the way ahead. The path can be seen contouring around from the Franz Senn Hütte into a steep, grey valley which it winds up, following a route to the high col in order to gain access to the huts and walks back in the main Stubai valley. The route in detail is described in Walk 16, suffice to say here that the ascent is increasingly gruelling, and that from the col it is most definitely worth the short walk on to the summit of the Basslerjoch before beginning the steep descent to the Neue Regensburger Hütte. This walk will take about 4 hours, even with an ascent of the Basslerjoch, so it represents a chance to rest in preparation for the next two days, which are a little harder.

One of the many types of sign found on the Horseshoe

The valley to the south-west of the Franz Senn Hütte

Our first goal on day four is the small, high level lake – Falbesoner See. The lake is easily reached via the Hohes Moos (high moss) and path 138, and it represents the start point for the first main climb of the day, up to a height of 2,880m (9,450ft), this is the col between the Nockwand and the Ruderhofspitze. From the col, a short descent leads to a long and undulating traverse line which weaves a way over ridges thrown down leg-like from higher peaks and across cold, grey glacier streams. An hour and half or so's walking leads to Hohe Grube (path junctions) and the Mutterberger See, another high level lake which shelters between the giant corrie walls of the Hölltalspitze and the Mutterberger Seespitze. From here, a short drop in height and you reach another contouring path which takes you across into the upper part of the Wilde Grube on path 135. Ahead lies the last climb before the Dresdner Hütte, and though it is steep in places, the magnificent surroundings will compensate and detach the mind from weary legs and heaving lungs. This last section is shared with Walk 20, which contains a description of the ascent and the subsequent drop down to the hut. You should allow approximately 5 – 6 hours for this part of the tour. You should take this opportunity to rest, eat and sleep well, for tomorrow you are really going to walk!

There is a total of around 8 hours walking today, over varied terrain which

The Pinnis valley – the last descent of the walk

137

The lower part of the valley

includes sharp ascents and descents, rocky traverses with fixed cables, good refreshment points and views as good as any you will see on this tour. It is a good idea to make an early start and get the first slog up to the Beiljoch done while it is still cool. This part of the journey is described in detail in Walk 20. The climb starts easily, becomes harder as it wends up a steep ridge, then eases as it approaches the col, resplendent with its many tall cairns and brilliant glacier views. The descent from the col is steep at first, then eases to give good walking down to the Sulzenauhütte and the first refreshment point.

The next section is again quite tough and is described in full in Walk 19. It takes you to the Nürnburger Hütte in about $2^1/_2$ hours, at which point you can again partake in a good variety of gastronomic delights if the fancy takes you. Now you are faced with the last stage of the day, the section to the Bremer Hütte. First travel south-east along varied paths and slabby rocks into the valley holding the Langtal stream which drains the Grübl glacier. Crossing the stream, the route then heads north-eastwards up and across the valley side before rounding a rocky section at the foot of a ridge (there are fixed cables here). Now work a way round into the upper Grübl cirque, and travel east-south-east across scree and moraine at the foot of the glacier. There is then a short, rocky ascent in a southerly direction up to the Simmingjochl at 2,764m (9,068ft). (There is a customs hut here – normally unmanned!) Path 102 then leads down steeply at first, then more gently in 45 minutes to the hut. Tonight's sleep will have been well earned.

The penultimate day, consists of a 6 hour walk predominantly along a high-level traverse line which takes the natural division between the ridges and steep corries of the south western end of the Habicht range and the steep, but smoother ground below. From the Bremer Hütte, the first landmark is the Lauterer See. The first part of the path is varied and includes easy sections over slabby rocks fixed with cable-ways. Cross the outflow of the See and continue easily until met by a path from the right. You are now faced with a short climb up on to the east ridge of the Aussere Wetterspitze. Reaching the saddle on the ridge involves some easy, but quite steep scrambling which has the inevitable fixed cables. Descending a little on the north side of the saddle, we are faced with a long traverse around and across a huge, broad basin which gives access to the south-east spur of the Ochsenkogel. The views by now are starting to really open up across on to the peaks on the opposite side of the Gschnitz valley, the Schneespitze – Weisswandspitze section looking especially impressive. A stony descent from the ridge, followed by an unwelcome, steep and grassy ascent leads to a col just to the west of the Pramarnspitze. The continuing traverse is relentless and tiring, but always blessed with good views and a wide variety of plant life which will be at its best in the early summer. Three major landmarks remain. First, the crossing of the wide corrie known as the Glattegrube, second the gap on the Alfeirkamm and third, the small lake which is only a short distance above the Innsbrucker Hütte. It's all downhill from here, so don't worry too much if you have a glass of wine too many tonight (unless you're going to nip up Habicht in the morning before the final descent!).

You will, hopefully, have spent a delightful and relaxing evening at the Innsbrucker Hütte and will be ready for the final day of the tour. It's a much less arduous day than the last two and consists of a descent of the Pinnis valley with its superbly situated Alms and high pastures. The descent is steep at first, but soon becomes progressively easier and takes a line which leads down into the valley bottom and the first hut, Karalm. Further down the valley, the Pinnisalm is in one of the loveliest settings imaginable. The valley bottom is flat and the flower-dotted meadows are verdant and surprizingly fertile considering their location. The river doesn't look much in good weather, but the extent of the river bed with its sprawling boulder fields gives a clue as to what it must be like in wet weather. To the right on descent are the huge limestone wall of the Ilmspitze and the Kirchdachspitze, a superb backdrop which has few peers in this area. The path down will probably become increasingly populated and is likely to be very busy when you get down as far as the Issenanger Alm. This is to a certain extent an intrusion as for the past few days the paths will have (hopefully) been relatively quiet, especially in the more remote areas. It is also an unavoidable intrusion and one which is found in every mountain area. However, hurry on past down to Neustift for some well-earned refreshment. It's a great feeling to relax at the end of a big walk and recall the best (and worst) bits, and to fix them permanently in your memory.

APPENDICES

I Glossary of Terms found in the Mountains

Alm	Mountain pasture, usually with one or two small huts
Arzt	Doctor
Ausser(er)	Outer
Bach	Stream
Baum	Tree
Berg	Mountain
Brucke	Bridge
Dorf	Village
Eis	Ice
Eisenbahn	Railway
Fluss	River
Friert	Freezing
Gasthof	Inn
Gefallen	Fallen
Gipfel	Peak
Gletscher/Ferner	Glacier
Grube	Hollow, Basin
Haus	House
Hinter(er)	Further, Rear
Inner(er)	Inner
Joch (Jochl)	Pass, Col
Kalt	Cold
Kar	Cirque
Klippe	Cliff
Leicht	Easy
Mittler(er)	Middle

Neblig	Foggy
Nieder	Gap, low point on a ridge
Notfall	Emergency
Regen	Rain
Scharte	Notch, gap, saddle in a ridge
Schnee	Snow
See	Lake
Sonnig	Sunny
Sturmisch	Stormy
Tal	Valley
Trocken	Dry
Uber	Over
Unfall	Accident
Unter	Under
Vorder(er)	Nearer, front
Wald	Forest
Warm	Warm
Wasserfal	Waterfall
Wechselhaft	Changeable
Weg	Path
Windig	Windy
Wolkig	Cloudy
Nord	North
Sud	South
Ost	East
West	West

II Common Signs

Abfahrt	Departures
Ausgang	Exit
Ausfahrt	Exit
Auskunft	Information
Damen	Ladies
Drucken	Push
Einfahrt/Eingang	Way in/Entrance
Eintritt	Admission
Fahrpreis	Fare
Frei	Free
Gefahr	Danger
Geschlossen	Closed
Getranke	Drink
Heiss	Hot
Herren	Men
Heir	Here
Kasse	Cash Desk
Kein...	No...
Nicht Rauchen	No Smoking
Nur Fur	Only for
Offen	Open
Privat	Private
Schwimmbad	Swimming Pool
Selbstbedienung	Self-service
Tag	Day
Trinkwasser	Drinking Water
Verboten	Forbidden
Verkehrsamt	Tourist Office
Voll	Full
Wechselstube	Bureau de Change
Ziehen	Pull

III Common Words and Phrases

Ich	I
Zie	You
Er	He
Sie	She
Sie	They
Miene	My
Habe	Have
Ist	Is
Sind	Are
Helfen	Help
Konnen Sei	Can you
Kann Ich Haben?	Can I have
Bitte	Please
Danke	Thank you
Bitte	You're welcome / Please
Ya	Yes
Nein	No
Guten Tag, or Tag, or in the mountains Gruss Gott	Hello
Morgen	Morning
Nacht	Night
Was Kostet Das	How much is that?
Konnen Sei Mir Helfen	Can you help me?
Ich Verstehe Nicht	I don't understand